BARRON'S
BUSINESS KEYS

KEYS TO UNDERSTANDING THE FINANCIAL NEWS

Third Edition

Nicholas G. Apostolou, D.B.A., C.P.A., D.A.B.F.A.
U. J. LeGrange Endowed Professor
Louisiana State University
Baton Rouge, Louisiana

D. Lawrence Crumbley, Ph.D., C.P.A., A.B.F.A.
KPMG Endowed Professor
Louisiana State University
Baton Rouge, Louisiana

BARRON'S

All inquiries should be addressed to:
Barron's Educational Series, Inc.
250 Wireless Boulevard
Hauppauge, NY 11788
http://www.barronseduc.com

Library of Congress Catalog Card Number 00-036282

International Standard Book Number 0-7641-1308-9

Library of Congress Cataloging-in-Publication Data

Apostolou, Nicholas G.
        Keys to understanding the financial news / Nicholas G. Apostolou, D.
    Larry Crumbley. — 3rd ed.
              p.   cm.
        Includes bibliographical references and index.
        ISBN 0-7641-1308-9
        1. Finance.   2. Newspapers — Sections, columns, etc. — Finance.
    I. Crumbley, D. Larry.   II. Title.

    HG173.A75   2000
    070.4'49332—dc21   00-036282
                                                                    CIP

PRINTED IN THE UNITED STATES OF AMERICA

9   8   7   6   5   4   3   2   1

CONTENTS

1

OVERVIEW OF THE NEWS

People are bombarded with financial and economic information on a daily basis. Reports on such items as the gross domestic product (GDP), unemployment rate, consumer price index, and the money supply are publicized not only in the financial news but also in our local newspapers. Anyone reading the financial pages is faced with a bewildering array of stock tables, price quotes, and predictions of future trends, often contradictory in nature. The concerned nonexpert may find it a daunting task to synthesize and integrate this information so as to make specific economic decisions.

This book is for those individuals who wish to understand the implications of the financial news. This understanding does not require you to be an expert. Rather, the goal is to permit you to make an informed appraisal of the information reported in local newspapers, in national financial newspapers such as the *Wall Street Journal* and *Investor's Business Daily,* on television, in weekly financial publications such as *Barron's,* in business periodicals such as *Business Week, Forbes,* and *Fortune,* and on the ever-expanding Internet sites.

This book is by no stretch of the imagination a theoretical treatment of finance, economics, or investments. For example, textbooks that deal with economics can be dull and forbidding, and they generally fail to provide elementary guidance on when economic information is reported and how you should interpret that information in making economic decisions.

Similarly, most finance and investment books are

1

either too theoretical or too personal, espousing the author's system of amassing riches. This book does not provide you with a foolproof system for becoming wealthy. Rather, it presents fundamental material from the areas of economics, finance, and investments to enable you to interpret the financial news with a little common sense and sophistication. In this way, you can form your own opinions about current economic and business events rather than looking for so-called experts to interpret them.

We are not suggesting that you dispense with expert advice. The point is to form your own opinion based upon the facts, so that you are better able to judge the validity of the advice of others. Otherwise, you don't have an independent check on other opinions.

The book is organized around Keys to understanding the financial news. The purpose of each of these discussions is to provide you with sufficient information to interpret the financial news and make economic decisions. It is a practical how-to book, rather than a theoretical or conceptual discussion. Internet sources are provided throughout this book. Specific examples are presented from the daily press to illuminate discussion of the Keys. Further, at the end of the book, a glossary is presented along with a series of the most commonly asked questions and answers to those questions.

2

COMMON STOCK

Common stock represents fractional shares of ownership in a corporation. Certain advantages make common stock an attractive investment:

1. *Liquidity:* Common stocks traded on stock exchanges can be quickly bought or sold at prices that are quoted in the financial press.
2. *Dividends:* Dividends are important to investors who desire ever-increasing income.
3. *Capital appreciation:* Many investors today are less interested in dividends than in seeing the price of the stock appreciate. The earnings not distributed to stockholders in dividends represent tax-deferred income. The reinvestment of profits should help the company earn greater profits in the future. Other things being equal, the greater the earnings or profits in the future, the more likely the stock will appreciate in price. Furthermore, taxes are not paid on gains until the stock is sold, and the gain may be taxed at a more favorable tax rate.

Exhibit 1 provides a graphic presentation of the returns from investment in common stocks, long-term corporate and government bonds, and Treasury bills, with a comparison of the increase in inflation over a 74-year period. Each of the series starts with a $1 investment at year-end 1925. Notice that common stocks were the big winners over the period 1926–1999 (a return of 11.3%).

The evidence is compelling that in the long run investments in common stock have outperformed investments in other capital markets. Although investors in common stock assume greater risk than those, for instance, who invest in corporate bonds, clearly the returns in the long run have been greater. Note also that although investments in the stocks of smaller corporations are riskier, their returns have exceeded the returns on blue-chip stocks.

EXHIBIT 1
Basic Series
Summary Statistics of Annual Returns
From 1926 to 1999

1/1/26 to 12/31/99

Asset Class	Geometric Mean	Arithmetic Mean	Standard Deviation
Large Company Stocks	11.3%	13.3%	20.1%
Small Company Stocks	12.6%	17.6%	33.6%
Long-Term Corporate Bonds	5.6%	5.9%	8.7%
Long-Term Government Bonds	5.1%	5.5%	9.3%
Intermediate-Term Government Bonds	5.2%	5.4%	5.8%
U.S. Treasury Bills	3.8%	3.8%	3.2%
Inflation	3.1%	3.2%	4.5%

Source: *Stocks, Bonds, Bills and Inflation: 2000 Yearbook,* Ibbotson Associates, Chicago, 2000

There is one caveat to investors: The returns from common stock investments listed in Exhibit 1 result from averaging the returns from many stocks. Poor choices of stocks can lead to losses even when the stock market is rising. During 1999, more stocks in the Dow Jones Industrial Average (DJIA) went down than went up. Thus, the successful investor must be willing to expend the time and effort to select quality stocks.

Recent History. The U.S. stock market entered the new millennium after finishing off its best decade in history. In the 1990s, the Dow Jones Industrial Average (see Key 6) was up 318%, by far its best performance. For the decade, the Nasdaq (see Key 4) was up a startling 795%, more than twice as much as the Dow. The Internet craze

4

was a principal reason that the Nasdaq index rose 85.6% in 1999, the best annual performance ever for a major American index.

What are the reasons for this brilliant performance? One suggested reason has been the subdued rate of inflation (see Key 16). Inflation averaged a lowly 2.9% in the 1990s, down from 5.1% in the 1980s and 7.4% in the 1970s.

Another reason was the dramatic improvement in productivity (see Key 21). Productivity growth in the late 1990s increased at almost twice the rate of productivity growth in the 1980s. Rising productivity meant reduced labor costs.

A third reason was the stellar growth in the U.S. economy. Year 2000 marks the tenth year of the current economic expansion. As of February 2000, this expansion became the longest in U.S. history. During this expansion, the economy generated more than 20 million jobs and $20 trillion in additional economic output. The last year of the decade produced an amazing performance: real GDP growth of more than 4%, unemployment at about 4%, and consumer price inflation of 2.7%.

3

STOCK EXCHANGES

Common stocks are traded primarily on nine stock exchanges in the United States. The largest stock exchange is the New York Stock Exchange (NYSE), whose list includes more than 3,000 companies with more than 260 billion shares issued and a market value of about $13 trillion. A smaller version of the NYSE is the American Stock Exchange (AMEX), which is also located in Manhattan's financial district and has now merged with the Nasdaq (see Key 4). These two are considered national exchanges.

Common stock is also traded on five major regional exchanges. The number of shares listed as well as the number of shares traded on the NYSE has increased steadily through the years. Prior to the 1960s, the average daily trading volume was less than 3 million shares. Daily volume averaged about 15 million shares during the first half of the 1970s and exceeded 30 million by the end of the decade. Volume exploded during the 1980s, with daily volume usually exceeding 100 million shares. In the 1990s, volume continued to surge with daily trading nearly a billion shares by the end of the decade.

Trading volume on the AMEX typically varies from 5% to 7% of that on the NYSE. The disparity between the activity on the two exchanges is greater when measured by the value of trading because the price of shares on the NYSE tends to be higher than that of shares on the AMEX.

Originally, regional exchanges traded the securities of the companies located in their areas—thus the origin of the name. However, the development of rapid communication expanded their scope. As a result, some stocks on the NYSE and AMEX are traded as well as local stocks.

The largest of the regional exchanges is the Chicago Stock Exchange, with trading activity now exceeding that of the AMEX. The Chicago Stock Exchange is now the second largest organized stock exchange in the United States.

Role of the Specialist. Stock exchange specialists are the center of the auction market for stocks. Their role is to maintain an orderly market for stocks. The specialist is a member of the exchange who has been assigned responsibility for about 15 different stocks. Currently, there are about 430 specialists on the NYSE.

In their effort to maintain fair and orderly markets in stocks assigned to them, specialists perform four distinct roles:

1. *Agent:* Specialists act as agent for other brokers on the floor.
2. *Dealer:* Specialists also are required to act as dealers, risking their capital whenever a temporary imbalance between buy and sell orders exists in any of their assigned stocks.
3. *Auctioneer:* In addition to quoting the current bid and ask price to other brokers, they also evaluate the orders they hold and establish a fair market price for each assigned stock at the beginning of each trading day.
4. *Catalyst:* Finally, specialists are supposed to serve as the market's catalysts, ensuring that orders in their assigned stocks move smoothly.

Listing. The requirements for listing on the NYSE are more stringent than the requirements on the other exchanges. A company must meet or exceed specified levels of net earnings, assets, and trading volume, and its shares must be widely held by investors. In addition, the NYSE requires evidence that trading interest in the company's shares is sufficient. Finally, a prospective listee also must agree to meet standards of disclosure, corporate governance, and stockholder participation.

4

OVER-THE-COUNTER MARKET

The term *over-the-counter* (OTC) originated when securities were traded over the counters in stores of various dealers from their inventory of securities. Currently, however, the term is a totally inaccurate description of how securities are traded in this market. The OTC market does not have a centralized trading floor where all orders are processed like the NYSE and AMEX. Instead, trading is conducted through a computer-telephone network linking dealers across the country. These systems allow dealers to deal directly with one another and with customers.

Securities Traded. The OTC market is a huge market including about 13,000 securities. Although OTC stocks represent many smaller, unseasoned companies, the actual range of securities traded is much greater than assumed. There are several reasons why some securities are represented in the OTC market rather than being listed on one of the exchanges. Some securities issued by smaller companies cannot meet the more stringent requirements of the exchanges. Unseasoned issues of smaller companies typically are traded in the OTC market.

In other cases, firms choose to have their securities traded in the OTC market even though they could fulfill the requirements for listing on the exchanges. These companies may wish to avoid the financial disclosure and reporting requirements required by the exchanges. Many large financial institutions continue to prefer to trade their securities in the OTC market.

Nasdaq. In 1971, the National Association of

Securities Dealers (NASD)—the organization of securities dealers that regulates the OTC markets—started providing stock price quotations through its National Association of Securities Dealers Automated Quotations (Nasdaq) system. This computerized communication network provides current bid and ask prices on about 6,000 securities. Through a terminal, a broker can instantly discover the bid and ask quotations of all dealers making a market in a stock. The broker can then contact the dealer offering the best price and negotiate a trade directly.

The Nasdaq has become the speculator's market of choice in recent years. Its stock market capitalization (price per share times number of shares outstanding) makes it the second largest securities market in the world, surpassed by only the New York Stock Exchange. However, its average share volume easily surpasses that of the New York Stock Exchange and currently is well over a billion shares a day.

The Nasdaq is dominated by high-technology companies, which comprise more than 70% of the market value of the index. Many of the initial public offerings (IPOs) (see Key 8) and Internet issues have zoomed upward in price trade on the Nasdaq. These stocks led the Nasdaq to its stunning 85.6% performance in 1999, which trounced the 25.22% gain of the DJIA and the 19.53% gain of the Standard & Poor's (S&P) 500.

Reading Nasdaq Quotes. Two lists of Nasdaq securities are published in newspapers. The principal list is called Nasdaq National Market Issues, which includes more than half of the stocks in the Nasdaq system. Inclusion is based upon a company's financial performance and investor interest in the stock. This list (Exhibit 2) shows actual transaction prices, like those shown for exchange-traded issues. The information presented is the same as that for NYSE and AMEX issues.

EXHIBIT 2

Nasdaq National Market Issues

52 Weeks Hi	52 Weeks Lo	Stock	Sym	Div	Yld %	PE	Vol 100s	Hi	Lo	Close	Net Chg
n 51 5/16	36	MCIWorldcm pf	WCOMP		...	...	1	51 5/16	51 5/16	51 5/16	...
n 37¾	16⅜	MCK Comm	MCKC		...	...	372	23½	21⅜	22½	– 1½
n 9¾	2 15/16	MCM Cap	MCMC		...	...	619	3⅞	3¼	3⅞	+ ½
14½	7⅜	♣ MDC A	MDCA		...	...	1114	9	8¼	8⅜	+ 1/16
26½	11⅜	MDSI Mobl	MDSI		...	...	219	25⅞	25	25¾	+ 5/16
39⅜	27¾	MECH Fnl	MECH	.80	2.3	14	114	34⅜	34 3/16	34 9/16	+ 9/16
32	8	META Gp	METG		...	26	99	19¼	19	19	...
23	14 15/16	MFB Cp	MFBC	.36	2.2	11	5	16 11/16	16 11/16	16 11/16	+ 1/16
12¼	5 13/16	♣ MFC Bcp g	MXBIF		...	...	250	8⅞	8 3/16	8⅞	...
5¾	2¾	♣ MFRI Inc	MFRI		...	27	50	4 5/16	4 5/16	4 5/16	...
n 10	9⅜	MFS Fnl	MFSF		...	...	492	9⅞	9⅝	9¾	+ ⅛
52¾	5 13/16	MGC Comm	MGCX		...	...	1230	50⅞	45	50¾	+ 2¾
14¾	7	♣ MGI Pharma	MOGN		...	80	183	12	11⅝	11 15/16	+ ¼
21⅞	2⅛	MH Meyersn	MHMY		...	10	1152	5 13/16	5⅛	5¼	– 7/16
n 75	18¼	MIH Ltd A	MIHL		...	...	1488	65⅜	56¾	59	+ 1
4⅝	1½	MIM Cp	MIMS		...	cc	1172	2 17/32	2¼	2 7/16	...
69	24½	MIPS Tch A	MIPS		...	83	1038	53	49¾	52	+ 1⅞
n 33¼	11⅞	MKS Instr	MKSI		...	...	1304	36½	32⅜	30⅛	+ 3⅛
57	11¾	MMC Ntwk	MMCN		...	86	4873	35	26¾	34⅜	+ 7⅝
13	6⅛	♣ MPW IndSvc	MPWG		...	13	131	7 15/16	7 9/16	7 15/16	+ ⅜
71⅝	5¾	MRV Comm	MRVC		...	dd	5208	63⅝	59⅝	62⅞	– 5/16
16 15/16	8½	♣ Minntch	MNTX	.10	1.0	10	66	10⅛	9⅝	9⅝	– ¼
13¾	7½	Minmanint	MMAN	.44	4.8	10	10	9⅛	9⅛	9⅛	– ¼
n 18 1/16	15	Mirae ADS	MRAE		...	...	5	16⅜	16⅜	16⅜	...
16¼	6 5/16	♣ MiravantMed	MRVT		...	dd	1057	9 9/16	9¼	9 5/16	– ¼
n 77⅝	16	MissnCrtcl	MCSW		...	...	685	72¼	67⅝	70	+ 2¾
36⅛	26	MS VlyBcsh	MVBI	.40	1.5	13	36	27¼	26⅞	27	+ ⅜
6¾	3 1/16	Mitchamind	MIND		...	dd	845	3 9/16	3¼	3 7/16	...
s 20¾	8 43/64	MityLite	MITY		...	19	22	15 27/32	15¼	15 9/16	...
4⅜	1 11/16	MobileAm	MAME	.11e	5.7	dd	72	2 1/16	1 15/16	1 15/16	– 1/16
23⅝	10¼	MobileMini	MINI		...	28	77	21½	20¾	21½	+ ½
24 7/16	3¼	♣ MobiusMgt	MOBI		...	cc	541	8⅛	7 11/16	7 15/16	+ 1/16
8½	4⅜	♣ MOCON	MOCO	.20	3.3	13	157	6	5¾	6	+ ⅛
n 79	17¾	MdmMedTysn	MMPT		...	dd	464	71	64 11/16	70⅜	+ 3⅜
▲ 245	71½	MdrnTimes	MTGNY		...	...	7	265	251	265	+ 20
38	23	♣ ModineMfg	MODI	.92	3.7	11	588	25 21/32	25	25	– ¾
18	4¾	Modtech	MODT		...	4	114	6¼	6	6	– ⅛
▲ 51½	19⅞	♣ MoleclrDvc	MDCC		...	68	125	52	47½	52	+ 2
57	25½	♣ Molex	MOLX	.10	.2	48	3248	57	56 5/16	56 11/16	– 3/16
46⅝	22½	♣ Molex A	MOLXA	.10	.2	41	1506	45¼	44½	45¼	– 3/16
n 25½	7	MomentBus A	MMTM		...	...	151	7⅞	7½	7⅞	+ 3/16
8 5/16	5	♣ MonrchCno	MCRI		...	44	30	5⅜	5¼	5¼	– ⅝

The other list covers issues that do not meet all the listing requirements (see Exhibit 3). Many of these smaller companies are eligible for the Nasdaq Small-Cap Issues list. Each listing includes the company name, dividend (if any), volume, closing price, and net change based on the previous close.

EXHIBIT 3
Nasdaq Small-Cap Issues

Issue Div	Vol 100s	Last	Chg
♣ DstFear	722	2⅛	− ⅟₁₆
DexterityS	271	1⁵⁄₁₆	− ⅟₁₆
DiaSys	160	11¾	...
DialCpA	363	6²⁷⁄₃₂	− ⅟₃₂
DialCp wt	222	2⅛	+ ⅛
DiehlG	34	7⅛	− ⅛
DigitOrgn	1867	12⅛	+ ¾
DigitRec	91	3⅞	+ ³⁄₁₆
DigVd wtA	1293	⁹⁄₁₆	...
... DigtlVid	61	10⅛	− ⅛
DiscGph n	311	3⅟₁₆	+ ³⁄₁₆
♣ DiscvLabs	490	2²⁹⁄₃₂	+ ¹¹⁄₃₂
♣ DscLb wtA	32	⅛	+ ⅟₁₆
DivrSnr	15	2⅛	...
Divrsnt g	5472	22	+ ½
DblEgl	20	3⅛	+ ⁵⁄₃₂
DrChina n	146	4½	− ½
♣ Gentnr	287	14	− ⅜
Geores	11	1⅛	...
GetgoMail	167	1⅛	...
GibbsCn	488	⁹⁄₁₆	+ ⅟₁₆
GibbsC wt	170	³⁄₃₂	...
GlasAire stk	143	5	+ 1¼
♣ GoldRs	301	1⁵⁄₁₆	...
GoldStd	28	1¼	− ⅛
GoldSt wt	304	6⁹⁄₃₂	+ ²²⁄₃₂
... GoldTri	7	2⁶⁄₆₄	− ⅟₆₄
GolfEnt	162	3¹⁄₃₂	+ ⁵⁄₃₂
GoodTm	24	2⅞	...
GoodrP pf .80	16	3½	+ ¼
GrndAdv	12	3⅛	− ⅛
GrndToy	1588	6½	+ ¼
GraphOn n	3235	18½	+ 4
GrOn wtA	105	14¹¹⁄₁₆	+ 5⁷⁄₁₆
Internt	700	3⁹⁄₁₆	+ ⁹⁄₁₆
IntrstHot n	27	3¼	...
IntrvstB n	111	6¼	...
IntrvisB	101	1⅜	+ ⁵⁄₁₆
Intrnet	1441	2¹³⁄₃₂	− ⅟₃₂
♣ InvRIEst n .51f	140	7⅛	− ⅜
Irvine	3037	2⅛	+ ⅛
Isomet	11	3⁹⁄₁₆	+ ⅛
Isramc	177	3⅞	+ ¼
IxysCp	335	6¼	+ ³⁄₁₆
JB Oxfrd	5464	7¹¹⁄₁₆	+ ⁵⁄₃₂
JLM Ctre	81	1⅜	− ¼
J2 Com	186	14¼	...
JksnvSB .30	1	8⅛	+ 2⅛
JadeFncl n	56	8¹³⁄₁₆	...
JanusHot n	4	2	+ ¼
Jenkonl	226	3¹³⁄₁₆	+ ⅟₁₆
NtiBnksh n	8	19¾	...
♣ NtlEnviro	42	2⅞	+ ¼
NatHme	161	1³⁄₁₆	+ ⅟₁₆
NtlWire	274	29¼	+ ¼
NatrHlth	2096	1⅜	− ¼
NeoMdia	239	4¼	+ ³⁄₃₂
NetLojix	963	2⁹⁄₁₆	+ ⅜
Netplex	1188	11⅛	− ⅟₁₆
Netsmrt	125	6⅜	+ ¼
NetSlint n	224	18⁵⁄₁₆	+ ⁵⁄₁₆
NetterD	38	1	+ ⅟₁₆
NtwkCn	203	5¼	+ ⁷⁄₃₂
NtwkSix	42	3⅜	+ ⅟₁₆
NetwSys n	154	3¾	+ ⅛
Network1	1459	10¹³⁄₁₆	+ 1⅟₁₆
♣ NetwNrth	123	1⅞	+ ⅟₁₆
NtrlPst n	68	1⁵⁄₁₆	...

11

5

STOCK TABLES

Stock tables summarize trading activity in individual securities. For example, composite results of the previous day's trading in stocks listed on the New York Stock Exchange and on five regional exchanges are found in the NYSE Composite Transactions table (see Exhibit 4). The table is typically found in the financial dailies and, sometimes in abbreviated form, in local newspapers, providing crucial information that should be evaluated before making a decision about investing in a stock.

The abbreviation "pf" indicates preferred stock. On the extreme left of some of the entries, abbreviations such as "s" are displayed. These abbreviations are explained in a section labeled "Explanatory Notes" located at the bottom of the page. For example, "s" denotes that a stock split or stock dividend of 25% or more occurred in the past 52 weeks. The explanatory notes apply to both NYSE- and AMEX-listed issues and Nasdaq securities. The shamrock symbol indicates that an annual report and current quarterly report, if available, can be obtained by calling 800-654-2582.

The first column in the table reports the highest price paid for the stock over the last 52 weeks, *excluding* the previous day's trading. The second column gives the lowest price paid over the last 52 weeks. The name of the company issuing the stock is given in the third column. Because of space considerations, abbreviations for company names are used. The majority of the securities listed refer to common stock. The final four columns on the right give the high, low, and closing prices for the day and the net change from the previous day. A ↑ at the extreme left denotes that the price is the highest traded over the last 52 weeks, while a ↓ at the extreme left indicates a new low for the previous 52 weeks. A separate table lists new highs and lows for each day of stocks listed on the exchange.

Other valuable information besides price is reflected in the table. Column 5, labeled "Div," is the annual cash dividend based upon the rate of the last quarterly payout. Extra dividends or stock dividends are indicated by appropriate footnotes. The next column provides the yield percentage, which is determined by dividing the cash dividend by the closing price of the stock.

The P/E, or price-earnings ratio, is computed by dividing the latest closing price by the latest available earnings per share (EPS), based on diluted EPS for the most recent four quarters. The P/E ratio is one of the most widely used measures for evaluating the price of a stock. This ratio cannot be used alone when making decisions but must be compared with the company's past P/E ratios and with the P/E ratios of similar companies. The P/E ratio may indicate how fast the market expects the company's earnings to grow. The higher the P/E ratio, the greater the potential growth in earnings should be.

Column 8 gives the number of shares traded in each stock, expressed in hundreds of shares. Thus, 75 means 7,500 shares were traded that day. Transactions generally take place in units of 100 shares, commonly called a round lot. A "z" before the volume figure means that the number represents the exact number of shares traded. Thus, "z75" means 75 shares were traded, not 7,500. When the number of shares traded is less than 100, it is commonly referred to as an odd lot.

EXHIBIT 4
New York Stock Exchange Composite Transactions

52 Weeks Hi	Lo	Stock	Sym	Div	Yld %	PE	Vol 100s	Hi	Lo	Close	Net Chg
26 1/16	22 1/4	MrgStn 8.20	un	2.05	8.9	...	49	23 3/16	23 1/16	23 1/8	...
11 7/16	7 3/16	MorsnKnud	MK			9	1065	7 15/16	7 9/16	7 13/16	− 1/16
5	1 7/8	MorsnKnud wt			...	...	175	2 5/16	2 1/16	2 5/16	+ 3/16
25 3/4	17 1/2	MorrisonMgt	MHI	.16	.7	19	117	21 11/16	21 9/16	21 9/16	− 1/16
20 11/16	13 ♣	MortnRestr	MRG			dd	13	15 1/2	15 3/8	15 1/2	...
13 1/4	6 3/8	Mossimo	MGX			dd	268	8 7/16	8	8 1/16	+ 7/16
n 25 3/16	19	MtrolaCap pfa	MOTA	1.67	8.4	...	427	20 3/8	19 1/2	19 3/4	+ 5/16
149 1/2	60 7/16 ♣	Motorola	MOT	.48	.3	cc	6222	148 1/2	147 1/16	147 1/4	− 5/8
36 15/16	19 7/16	MuellerInd	MLI			16	762	36 1/4	35 3/16	36 1/4	+ 5/16
14 5/16	10 3/4	Muniassets	MUA	.81e	7.4	...	554	11 1/16	10 3/4	11	+ 1/8
14 1/2	11 5/16	MuniAdvntg	MAF	.80	6.9	...	261	11 5/8	11 7/16	11 9/16	+ 1/16
9 5/16	7 1/16 ♣	MuniHilnco	MHF	.58	7.8	...	1172	7 7/16	7 5/16	7 7/16	...
21 1/8	16 3/4 ♣	MuniMtgEq	MMA	1.62f	8.8	11	113	18 1/2	18 3/8	18 1/2	+ 1/8
14 1/8	10 9/16	MuniPrtnrs	MNP	.80	7.3	...	425	11	10 15/16	10 15/16	+ 3/16
13 1/2	10 3/4	MuniPrtnrsII	MPT	.75	6.7	...	79	11 1/4	11 1/8	11 13/16	...
12 7/16	8 3/4	MunienFd	MEN	.64e	7.1	...	2870	9 1/8	8 13/16	9 1/16	+ 1/8
16 9/16	11 7/16	MuniHldgsCA	CLH	.84e	7.1	...	486	11 13/16	11 11/16	11 13/16	+ 1/8
▼ 15 1/2	11 7/16	MuniHldgCA II	MUC	.82e	6.9	...	1225	11 13/16	11 5/8	11 13/16	+ 5/16
15 5/8	10 1/2	MuniHldgCA III	MCF	.80e	7.1	...	517	11 5/8	11 1/4	11 1/4	+ 5/16
n 15 5/8	10 7/16	MuniHldgCA IV	CIL	.67e	6.0	...	1183	11 5/16	10 5/8	11 1/4	+ 7/16
n 15 15/16	11 5/8	MuniHldgCA V	CAF	.28e	2.3	...	185	12 7/16	12	12 1/4	+ 3/16
16 11/16	12 5/16 ♣	NuvinsCA	NPC	.86a	6.4	...	43	13 1/2	13 3/8	13 3/8	− 1/16
15 11/16	11 5/8	NuvinsCA2	NCL	.80a	6.8	...	322	11 13/16	11 5/8	11 11/16	− 1/4
15 15/16	12 11/16	NuvinsCA TxF	NXC	.79a	6.2	...	100	12 13/16	12 3/4	12 13/16	...
15 7/8	12 3/8	NuvinsFL	NFL	.80	6.3	...	158	13	12 3/4	12 3/4	− 1/8
16 13/16	11 1/2	NuvinsMuni	NIO	.89	7.3	...	2889	12 1/4	11 7/8	12 1/4	+ 1/4
16 1/2	12 1/2	NuvNY Prm	NNF	.83	6.6	...	106	12 5/8	12 1/2	12 5/8	− 1/16
15 1/2	12 1/4	NuvNY TxF	NXN	.78	6.2	...	80	12 11/16	12 1/2	12 1/2	− 1/8
14 3/8	10 1/8	NuvinsPrm2	NPX	.73	7.1	...	1386	10 7/16	10 3/16	10 1/4	− 1/16
16 1/4	11 13/16 ♣	NuvinsQual	NQI	.92	7.0	...	1321	13 1/4	12 7/8	13 3/16	+ 1/4
16 3/16	11 1/2 ♣	NuvinvQual	NQM	.92a	7.9	...	1308	11 13/16	11 5/8	11 11/16	+ 1/8
16 3/16	11 13/16	NuvMD Prm	NMY	.78	6.4	...	45	12 1/8	12	12 1/8	...
17 1/16	14	NuvMA Prm	NMT	.85	6.1	...	131	14 1/16	14	14	− 1/16
15 3/4	11 11/16	NuvMl Prm	NMP	.83	7.0	...	143	11 15/16	11 3/4	11 15/16	+ 3/16
17 9/16	12 1/2	NuvMl Qual	NUM	.92a	7.3	...	306	12 15/16	12 11/16	12 11/16	− 1/8
16 11/16	11 15/16	NuvMunAdv	NMA	.96	8.0	...	2296	12 1/8	11 15/16	12	− 1/16
12 5/16	9 7/8	NuvMuniInco	NMI	.69a	6.6	...	89	10 9/16	10 7/16	10 1/2	− 1/16
16 11/16	11 7/16	NuvMuniMkt	NMO	.97	7.9	...	1089	12 1/4	12 1/16	12 1/4	+ 1/16
9 15/16	7 11/16 ♣	NuvValue	NUV	.51a	6.5	...	4705	7 7/8	7 3/4	7 7/8	...
17 9/16	12 3/16 ♣	NuvNJ Inv	NQJ	.92a	7.3	...	306	12 5/8	12 1/2	12 5/8	− 1/16
16 13/16	11 3/4	NuvNJ Prm	NNJ	.86	7.0	...	361	12 7/16	12 1/4	12 5/16	...
n 15 1/8	11 13/16	NuveenNY	NAN	.86	7.0	...	600	12 7/16	12 1/8	12 5/16	+ 1/16

In the *Wall Street Journal* some of the quotations are boldfaced, which highlights those issues with price changes of 5% or more from their previous closing price. Underlined quotations indicate those stocks with large changes in volume compared with the issue's average trading volume. The underlined quotations are for the 40 largest volume percentage leaders on the NYSE and the Nasdaq system. On the AMEX, underlined quotations

14

highlight the 20 largest volume percentage gainers. Both of these features alert investors to stocks that may be of interest.

Investor's Business Daily provides three key items in its stock tables not available in any other newspaper:

1. *EPS Rank* measures a company's short- and long-term earnings-per-share growth rate and the stability of that growth.
2. *Rel Str* stands for relative price strength and measures each stock's relative price change daily over the last 12 months compared with all other stocks in the table.
3. *Vol % Chg* shows a stock's trading volume for that day in terms of its percentage change above or below the stock's average daily volume for the last 50 trading days.

6

MARKET AVERAGES AND INDEXES

The Dow Jones Industrial Average (DJIA) is the stock market average most widely followed by the general public. The index was first calculated by Charles Dow in 1884 by adding together the prices of 11 important stocks and dividing the total by 11. The average was broadened in 1928 to include 30 stocks, and the composition of companies has been updated over the years. The corporations represented in the index have always been large "blue-chip" companies. The divisor is no longer equal to the number of stocks in the index because it has been changed frequently to compensate for stock splits, stock dividends, and other factors.

Although the DJIA continues to be the most publicized index, there also are Dow Jones indexes for 20 transportation-company stocks (Dow Jones Transportation Index) and 15 utility-company stocks (Dow Jones Utilities Index), as well as a composite index of the 65 stocks in the three indexes. The names of the stocks included in these indexes are printed each day in the *Wall Street Journal*.

On October 26, 1999, Dow Jones announced that Microsoft, Intel, Home Depot, and SBC Communications would join the DJIA on November 1, replacing Chevron, Sears, Union Carbide, and Goodyear. This action was taken to increase the representatives of high technology in the Dow and address criticism of the Dow that it had become too stodgy and dowdy. The move was unusual in that Microsoft and Intel are the first Dow industrials not to trade on the New York Stock Exchange. They both trade on the Nasdaq.

The addition of Microsoft and Intel doubles the number of tech stocks from two to four. The two already there are IBM and Hewlett-Packard. Still, the four stocks account for only 16% of the Dow's weighting in the Standard & Poor's 500 Stock Index.

The Dow Jones stock averages are price weighted, meaning that the component stock prices are added together and the result is divided by another figure called the divisor. As a result, a high-priced stock has a greater effect on the index than a low-priced stock. In other words, a stock whose price is $100 per share is going to affect the index more than a stock whose price is $30. A significant fluctuation in the price of one or several of the stocks in the index can distort the average; however, over the long term, the DJIA has been an effective indicator of the direction of the overall market.

Dow Jones publishes in the *Wall Street Journal* a Stock Market Data Bank, which appears daily on page C2. Besides the Dow Jones Averages, there are the New York Stock Exchange indexes of all stocks traded on the exchange, and the NYSE indexes of major sectors. For each index, the Data Bank discloses the latest day's closing value and changes from the previous day, a year earlier, and the end of the previous year, both in absolute terms and as a percentage of the previous figure. Also shown are the Nasdaq, AMEX, the 1,700-stock Value Line, and the Wilshire indexes (see Exhibit 5).

A widely publicized theory using the Dow Jones indexes is the Dow theory, which tries to predict reversals and trends in the market. Dow theorists seek to detect the primary trend in stock prices. Primary trends are the bear (declining) and bull (rising) markets. Secondary movements last only a few months and are usually called corrections. Most Dow theorists do not believe that the emergence of a new primary trend has occurred until a move in the Dow Jones Industrial Average is confirmed by a similar move in the Dow

Jones Transportation Average. A primary trend is not confirmed until both Dow Jones indexes reach new highs or lows. If this event does not occur, the market will return to its former trading range. Although Dow theorists often disagree on when a true breakout has occurred, the theory does provide a commonsense approach to guiding investors in distinguishing between bull and bear markets.

Standard & Poor's Indexes. Standard & Poor's indexes are weighted in proportion to the market value of the stocks in the index. S&P has six weighted indexes:

1. S&P 500 Stock Index (also called the Composite Index)
2. S&P 400 Stock Index (also called the Industrials Index)
3. S&P 600 SmallCap Index
4. S&P Utility Stock Index
5. S&P 1500 Super Composite Index
6. S&P 400 MidCap Index

All these indexes are assigned values of 10 for the base period of 1941–1943.

The S&P 500 is the most widely followed barometer of stock market movements by market professionals. Originally, it was computed with a sample of 233, but in 1957 it assumed a sample size of 500 stocks. On a daily basis, its movement is more representative of the movement of the stock market as a whole because of its larger sample size and the fact that the index is market weighted. The S&P 500 is made up of 400 industrial, 20 transportation, 40 utility, and 40 financial stocks. The index consists primarily of NYSE-listed companies with some AMEX and Nasdaq stocks. The S&P 500 is the basis for a widely traded index option (see Key 12).

NYSE Composite Index. The New York Stock Exchange introduced the NYSE Composite Index in 1966. This broad-based index measures the changes in the aggregate market value of all NYSE common stocks.

The market value of each stock is obtained by multiplying its price per share by the number of listed shares. The sum of the individual market shares, the aggregate market value, is then expressed relative to a base market value of $50—a figure approximating the average price of all common stocks on the base date of December 31, 1965. If the index stands at 600, that means the average value of all common stock listed on the NYSE on that date is 12 times as much as it was on December 31, 1965.

As shown in Exhibit 5, the NYSE also computes group indexes for industrial, utility, transportation, and financial stocks. These indexes are computed in the same way as the NYSE Composite Index, although a smaller number of issues are included.

Other Indexes. The American Stock Exchange Composite Index is computed in much the same way as the NYSE index. It measures the performance of 800 issues on the AMEX. The base value of 50 is based on the close of trading on August 31, 1973, when this index was first introduced.

EXHIBIT 5–Stock Market Data Bank 1/3/00

Major Indexes	†12-Mo High	Low	Daily High	Daily Low	Close	Net Chg	%	†12-Mo Chg	% Chg	From 12/31 Chg	% Chg
Dow Jones Averages											
30 Industrials	11497.12	9120.67	11522.01	11305.69	11357.51	− 139.61	− 1.21	+2173.24	+ 23.66	− 139.61	− 1.21
20 Transportation	3783.50	2808.44	2996.28	2922.21	2943.51	− 33.53	− 1.13	− 173.98	− 5.58	− 33.53	− 1.13
15 Utilities	333.45	269.20	283.16	275.91	x276.71	− 6.65	− 2.35	− 35.20	− 11.29	− 6.65	− 2.35
65 Composite	3366.13	2831.53	3216.98	3156.13	x3170.20	− 44.18	− 1.37	− 305.48	− 10.66	− 44.18	− 1.37
DJ Global-US	1390.32	1153.87	1439.21	1355.09	1379.03	− 11.29	− 0.81	+ 211.43	+ 18.11	− 11.29	− 0.81
New York Stock Exch.											
Composite	663.12	576.17	650.35	635.93	639.52	− 10.78	− 1.66	+ 45.40	+ 7.64	− 10.78	− 1.66
Industrials	828.21	722.97	828.51	812.51	818.25	− 9.96	− 1.20	+ 77.42	+ 10.45	− 9.96	− 1.20
Utilities	518.74	426.40	511.99	501.53	505.59	− 5.56	− 1.09	+ 61.49	+ 13.85	− 5.56	− 1.09
Transportation	560.33	428.31	469.34	455.64	459.47	− 7.23	− 1.55	+ 16.52	+ 3.47	− 7.23	− 1.55
Finance	584.22	457.63	516.62	496.23	496.82	− 19.79	− 3.83	+ 25.95	+ 4.96	− 19.79	− 3.83
Standard & Poor's Indexes											
500 Index	1469.25	1212.19	1478.00	1438.36	1455.22	− 14.03	− 0.95	+ 227.12	+ 18.49	− 14.03	− 0.95
Industrials	1841.92	1461.72	1853.64	1810.03	1835.37	− 6.60	− 0.36	+ 358.72	+ 24.29	− 6.60	− 0.36
Utilities	269.98	215.62	227.22	220.68	221.31	− 5.91	− 2.60	+ 38.37	+ 14.78	− 5.91	− 2.60
400 MidCap	444.67	353.14	446.49	431.43	438.13	− 6.54	− 1.47	+ 49.09	+ 12.62	− 6.54	− 1.47
600 SmallCap	197.79	154.83	198.96	191.74	194.31	− 3.48	− 1.76	+ 17.90	+ 10.15	− 3.48	− 1.76
1500 Index	308.89	255.39	310.65	302.15	305.76	− 3.13	− 1.01	+ 46.14	+ 17.77	− 3.13	− 1.01
Nasdaq Stock Market											
Composite	4131.15	2208.05	4192.19	3989.71	4131.15	+ 61.84	+ 1.52	+1923.10	+ 87.09	+ 61.84	+ 1.52
Nasdaq 100	3790.55	1854.39	3836.86	3643.25	3790.55	+ 82.72	+ 2.23	+1936.16	+ 104.4	+ 82.7	+ 2.2
Industrials	2286.52	1294.40	2303.53	2197.65	2286.52	+ 47.55	+ 2.12	+ 982.13	+ 75.29	+ 47.55	+ 2.12
Insurance	2372.33	1702.46	1901.66	1848.65	1857.11	+ 39.17	+ 2.07	+ 42.07	+ 2.32	+ 39.17	+ 2.07
Banks	1898.49	1687.70	1630.02	1623.61	1630.02	− 61.27	− 3.62	− 208.15	− 11.32	− 61.27	− 3.62
Computer	2368.82	1151.80	2391.90	2278.11	2368.82	+ 43.42	+ 1.87	+1217.02	+ 105.6	+ 43.4	+ 1.8
Telecommunications	1023.45	498.84	1054.18	995.06	1023.45	+ 8.05	+ 0.79	+ 524.61	+ 105.1	+ 8.5	+ 0.7
Others											
Amex Composite	876.97	683.61	879.47	861.39	878.74	+ 8.23	+ 0.94	+ 185.13	+ 27.08	+ 8.23	+ 0.94
Russell 1000	767.97	632.53	772.82	752.92	761.52	+ 6.45	+ 0.84	+ 119.74	+ 18.66	+ 6.45	+ 0.84
Russell 2000	504.75	383.37	510.96	489.95	496.42	+ 8.33	+ 1.65	+ 75.16	+ 17.84	+ 8.33	+ 1.65
Russell 3000	793.31	652.13	798.42	776.40	786.20	+ 7.11	+ 0.90	+ 123.04	+ 18.55	+ 7.11	+ 0.90
Value-Line (geom.)	472.95	398.58	432.33	422.29	424.19	− 6.85	− 1.59	− 13.68	− 3.12	− 6.85	− 1.59
Wilshire 5000	13812.67	11146.59	...	...	13710.46	− 102.21	− 0.74	+2403.26	+ 21.25	− 102.21	− 0.74

†-Based on comparable trading day in preceding year.

20

The Nasdaq indexes have become widely followed recently because of increasing interest in high-technology stocks, which dominate the index. The Nasdaq Composite Index is market weighted and covers about 6,000 stocks. The Nasdaq also publishes several specialized group indexes covering specific industries.

The Wilshire 5000 Equity Index was first introduced in 1974 to meet the need for an index that reflects the performance of the organized exchanges as well as of the OTC markets. This index of 7,200 (not 5,000) stocks is the broadest index and thus is the most representative of movements in the overall market. This index is calculated in the same manner as the S&P 500 and the NYSE Composite Indexes, with a base value of 1,404.595 on December 31, 1980. In 1999, its high exceeded 13,000, indicating that the stocks in the index had gone up almost tenfold in about twelve years.

7

BUYING AND SELLING STOCKS

Before buying and selling stock, one must establish an account with a broker. Brokers, also known as account executives or registered representatives, are required by law to carry out their clients' investment decisions efficiently and professionally. To select a broker, check with family and friends or a trusted banker, lawyer, or accountant. Like other professionals, some brokers service their customers better than others do. Before making a final decision, arrange for a full interview to discuss the firm's procedures and rates and evaluate whether this broker can best fulfill your needs and objectives. In the interview, don't be afraid to ask hard questions; and if the answers are not satisfactory, shop elsewhere.

Types of Brokers. Brokers formerly were divided into two types: discount brokers and full-service brokers. Discount brokers usually limit their services to buying and selling securities for investors who know precisely what they want. Their function is not to give advice about the securities their clients are considering. As a result, their commission rates are generally less than half of those charged by full-service brokers.

Full-service brokers, such as Merrill Lynch, can provide information about the securities of companies. They generally maintain a research department that provides information to its brokers upon request. In addition, the research department issues recommendations about favored stocks and provides forecasts of future market trends.

The Internet is blurring the traditional distinction between full-service and discount firms. The fastest growing segment of the brokerage industry involves firms engaged in online trading. Online trading has had a revolutionary impact on the way stocks are sold. Trades often are executed at a cost of 5% of what a traditional broker would charge (as low as $5 for a trade of 1,000 shares). The cost and ease of execution account for the fact that 30% of trades are currently being handled online.

The explosion of interest in online investing finally forced the hand of the largest full-service firm, Merrill Lynch. On June 1, 1999, Merrill Lynch announced that it would let its customers trade via the Internet for as little as $29.95 per trade, the same as its rival, Charles Schwab, starting December 1, 1999. However, many of its customers want the advice of a broker, so Merrill Lynch is hoping that they will prefer a fee-based, full-service plan that charges a minimum of $1,500 for unlimited trades and a broker's counsel. The fee will equal 1% of stock and mutual fund assets and 0.3% of cash and bond holdings.

Opening an Account. Opening an account with a brokerage firm is not significantly different from opening a bank account. One has to provide a name, address, occupation, social security number, citizenship, a suitable bank or financial reference, and an acknowledgment that the customer is of legal age. Most investors open *cash accounts*, meaning they will settle transactions promptly without credit. *Margin accounts* are used when customers wish to use borrowed funds to supplement their own commitment. The customer makes only partial payment for the securities and borrows the rest from a broker. These margin accounts are better suited to more experienced investors prepared to assume additional risks.

Placing an Order. When you decide to buy or sell stock, you contact your broker and ask for a quote on your stock. The quote consists of two numbers telling you the highest price anyone currently is willing to pay and the lowest price at which anyone is willing to sell the stock. Several choices can be made. You might place either a *market order*, which means you will receive the best available price at the time an order is executed, or a *limit* order, which means the trade can only be executed at a specific price. If a limit order is placed, it can apply for that day only or else be "open" or "good till canceled," which means that the order is applicable until executed or until you cancel it. An online trade is handled in a similar fashion on your computer and can be completed in seconds.

An order for an exchange-listed stock probably enters an electronic pathway. New York Stock Exchange issues will generally be processed by a computer system called SuperDot that processes orders and reports back to the broker in an average of 22 seconds. On the day following the trade, the brokerage firm can send a written confirmation and bill to the client.

8

INITIAL PUBLIC OFFERINGS (IPOs)

An IPO occurs when a company offers stock for sale to the public for the first time. Typically, the company is small and growing and needs to raise money for further expansion.

The IPO market in 1999 was a frenzy of activity. In the biggest bull market ever for IPOs, about a quarter of the 544 IPOs at least doubled from their offering price on their first day of trading. In 1998, only 3%, or 12, of the 362 IPOs doubled the first day, and that was a record. Only three IPOs doubled between 1990 and 1995, and only seven managed to do so in the 1980s. IPOs raised $69.1 billion in 1999, the most in history, and the year also witnessed the largest IPO ever—UPS (which raised $5.5 billion).

Some of the first-day gains were astounding. VA Linux Systems, which sells computers that run a free operating system, registered and eye-popping first day gain of 698%. Linux was initially offered at $30 a share, but surging demand caused the price to explode to $239.25 by the end of the first day. It was the first time an IPO on the Nasdaq finished its first day above $200 a share. Incredibly, the market capitalization (price per share times number of shares outstanding) was $9.5 billion for a company that in its previous quarter reported revenues of $14.8 million and a loss of $15 million.

Companies initially sell stock to the public by calling upon investment bankers to act as underwriters. An investment banking firm is a firm specializing in arranging financing for companies by finding investors to buy newly issued shares. Underwriters assume the risk of buying newly issued securities from a company and reselling them to investors.

Before shares can be sold to the public, the offering must first receive an approved registration with the Securities and Exchange Commission (SEC). The SEC is the government agency charged with regulating the securities industry. The SEC requires the preparation of a prospectus, a legal document containing a detailed account of the company's financial position, its operations, and investment plans for the future.

While waiting for SEC approval, the investment banker circulates a preliminary prospectus among investors to generate interest in the stock offering. This document is commonly called a red herring because of the red ink that denotes its preliminary status. The preliminary prospectus does not include the final offering price. This price is not set because market conditions might change while the SEC approval is being sought. Upon SEC approval, the prospectus will be updated, and the underwriter can begin selling the company's shares to investors.

Wall Street syndicate managers estimate that institutions get to buy about 60% of the typical IPO deal and 80% of the hot deals. In a normal deal, individuals might be allocated 25% of the shares, whereas in an exciting offering they might be lucky to get 5% of the shares. After the institutions rake in their shares, there is not much to divvy up among individuals. Unfortunately, the way the system works is that the easiest offerings for individuals to participate in are those the institutions do not want to touch. These offerings are often of dubious quality.

Investors new to the IPO game should be aware of the performance history of their potential investment. Research has shown that, in the long run, most IPOs end up underperforming the larger market. Most IPOs historically fail to beat major market indexes; typically, they start to falter six months after their IPO, because many of the institutions "flip" the purchased stock after the initial run-up.

Even in 1999, a record year for IPOs, when the Nasdaq climbed 85.6%, there were many losers. Of the 544 IPOs offered that year, about half were Internet-related and many realized phenomenal first-day returns. However, by the end of the year, more than 22% were selling below their IPO price. Expect the same fate to occur to many of the others if the market falters.

Investors should be cautious about the IPO market. At some point, when the IPO market is hot, supply will always overwhelm demand. For those wishing to speculate, wait about two weeks after the offering price before buying. This hiatus lets enthusiasm subside but still lets the investor buy the stock before Wall Street analysts issue their first, usually positive, company reports. The SEC requires underwriters to wait 25 days (called the quiet period) after the stock begins trading before commenting on the offering.

Information on IPOs can be obtained at *www.ipo.com* or *www.herring.com.*

9

SHORT SALES

Most investors purchase stock with the expectation that a profit will be made from a rise in the price of the stock. However, investors have an alternative way of generating a profit when they believe that a stock is overpriced and expect it to decline in the future: a short sale. A short sale is the sale of a security that is not owned with the intention of repurchasing it later at a lower price. The investor borrows the security from another investor through a broker and sells it in the market. Subsequently, the investor will repurchase the security and return the security to the broker.

Most brokers will handle all arrangements on behalf of the investor. Usually a broker has other clients who own the security and are willing to loan shares.

An important aspect of a short sale order is that an investor does not receive the proceeds of the order at the time the trade is executed. In a short sale, the money is kept by the brokerage firm until the short is covered, that is, until the security is purchased and returned to the lender. Furthermore, to ensure that the short position will be covered, the broker requires the posting of collateral. Most short selling is done through margin accounts, in which case short sellers are required to have in their accounts a required percentage of the stock's price.

Short selling is a legitimate investment technique, but it should only be used by the well-informed. When a stock is purchased outright, the maximum loss is the price of the stock. With short selling, the sky is the limit for losses because a stock's price has no ceiling. The riskiness of short selling demands extra diligence in monitoring the position.

Reports on the total number of shares sold short of stocks listed on the New York and American stock exchanges, as well as on the Nasdaq, are disclosed soon after the middle of each month in the financial press and on various web sites. A large short position in a stock is not necessarily a bearish or pessimistic indicator, according to many analysts. In fact, technical analysts frequently regard a large short position to be bullish. They theorize that a significant pent-up demand exists for the stock among the short sellers, who ultimately will have to purchase shares to pay back their borrowed stock. In such a case, a sudden buying rush is possible if the stock's price increases and investors have to cover their shorts.

Specialist Short Sales. As part of their effort to maintain an orderly market, specialists regularly engage in short selling. However, they also have some discretion when they feel strongly about market changes. Technicians who want to follow the smart money (specialists are assumed to be smart) attempt to determine what the specialist is doing and act accordingly. When specialist short sale ratio (specialist short sales relative to total short sales) is low, this condition is considered a sign that specialists are bullish and are attempting to avoid short selling. When the ratio surges, specialists are assumed to be bearish. Short sales by specialists are reported weekly in the *Wall Street Journal, Investor's Business Daily*, and *Barron's.*

Technical Points. Two technical points relevant to short sales are important. First, a short sale can only be made on an uptick. In other words, execution can occur only after an increase of 1/8 of a point or more in the security's price. This restriction was implemented to prevent traders from forcing a profit on a short sale by pushing the price down by continually selling short. Second, a short seller is responsible for the dividends to the investor who loaned the stock. The purchaser of the stock sold short receives the dividend from the corporation. As a result, the short seller must pay the same amount to the investor who loaned the stock.

An excellent book to help with identifying prospects for shorting is *The Act of Short Selling* by Kathryn F. Staley (John Wiley & Sons, 1997).

10

THE SECURITIES AND EXCHANGE COMMISSION

Prior to the Great Depression of the 1930s, the federal government did little to regulate the securities markets. However, the depression resulted in the virtual collapse of the securities markets, fostering widespread criticism of their operation. In an effort to restore confidence in their operation, Congress intervened and established the Securities and Exchange Commission (SEC) to administer federal laws that seek to provide protection for investors. The overriding purpose of these laws is to ensure the integrity of the securities markets by requiring full disclosure of material facts related to securities offered to the public for sale.

Securities Act of 1933. This act provides for the regulation of the initial public distribution of a corporation's securities. The SEC requires a registration statement, which includes such information as

1. A description of the registrant's properties and business
2. A description of significant provisions of the security to be offered for sale and its relationship to the registrant's other capital securities
3. Information about the management of the registrant
4. Financial statements certified by independent public accountants

The SEC does not insure investors against losses. Nor

31

does it prevent the sale of securities in risky, poorly managed, or unprofitable companies. Rather, registration with the SEC is designed to provide adequate and accurate disclosure of required material facts about the company and securities proposed to be sold. A portion of the information contained in the registration statement is included in a prospectus that is prepared for public distribution.

The Securities Exchange Act of 1934. This act provides protection to investors by regulating the trading of securities of publicly held companies in the secondary market. Continuous disclosure of company activities is required through annual, quarterly, and special reports. Form 10-K is the annual report, which contains a myriad of financial data in addition to nonfinancial information such as the names of the corporate officers and directors and the extent of their ownership. Form 10-Q is the quarterly report, which contains abbreviated financial and nonfinancial information. Form 8-K is a report of material events or corporate changes deemed of importance to the shareholders or to the SEC. All of these can be obtained on the SEC's web site, *www.sec.gov*, private SEC sites such as *www.freeedgar.com*, and SEC links on almost any investment site, such as Yahoo! Finance at *quote.yahoo.com*.

11

INSIDER TRADING

Insider trading abuses have received wide publicity in recent years. Michael Milken, for instance, was sentenced to prison and fined over $500 million. An insider is basically a person with access to significant information before it is released to the public. The SEC has been very active in pressing cases against insiders in an effort to prevent them from benefiting at the public's expense from information available only to them.

Insider Trading Sanctions Act of 1984. Insider trading sanctions are designed to prevent the misuse of confidential information not available to the general public. Examples of such misuse are buying and selling of securities based on nonpublic information or relaying the information to others so that they may buy or sell securities before this information is available to the public. The SEC has a broad definition of insiders, ranging from corporate directors, officers, and executives to clerks who photocopy confidential information. All insider trading is not illegal. The officers and directors of a company may buy and sell shares of that company as long as they do not do so on the basis of information that is concealed from the public. However, the SEC requires all these people, as well as owners of more than 10% of a company's stock, to file a report showing their holdings of the company's stock. Subsequently, they must file reports for any month where there was any change in those holdings. These insider reports are made public and are widely reported in the financial press. In addition, several newsletters use these reports as a primary basis for their recommendations.

Using the authority given it under the Securities

Exchange Act of 1934, the SEC has brought numerous civil actions in federal court against persons accused of insider trading. In addition, the SEC has been a strong supporter of legislation to increase the penalties against those accused of insider trading. The Insider Trading Sanctions Act of 1984 allows the imposition of fines up to three times the profit gained by the use of insider information.

The Internet is the best source of information on insider activity. Both Yahoo Finance (*quote.yahoo.com*) and Bloomberg (*quote.bloomberg.com*) provide extensive disclosure on insider transactions. For those investors who want a more detailed analysis, Insider Trader (*www.insidertrader.com*) costs $49 per year.

Using Insider Data. Logically, insiders should have superior knowledge of the real value of their company. Corporate insiders should be better informed about the company's current business activities and future prospects than either stockholders or security analysts. Although they cannot legally purchase shares based upon material, nonpublic information, they can purchase stock based upon their perception that the intrinsic worth of the stock exceeds the current market price.

A further legal provision limiting the ability of insiders to speculate in the stock of their own company has significant implications for investors. Company insiders are prohibited from selling shares after the initial public offering for 180 days (called the lockup period). Any profit from the purchase or sale of the stock realized within the lockup period can be claimed by the company.

Although several market forecasters use total insider activity to anticipate broad stock market movements (available in *Barron's* weekly), the relationship between total insider buying and selling and the changes in the overall market is rather tenuous. For example, indicators of insider activity would be considered neutral to bullish prior to the crash of October 1987. However, insider data do provide useful clues about the prospects of an individual company. Several academic studies have found that stocks bought by insiders outperform the market.

Martin Zweig, a prominent investment adviser, believes an insider-buy signal occurs when three or more insiders have bought and none have sold a stock within the most recent three-month period. Conversely, he believes an insider-sell signal occurs when three or more insiders sell and none buy within that same period. Insider-sell signals are not as accurate as insider-buy signals, because insiders may sell stocks for tax or other reasons not related to their perceptions of how well or how poorly their company is doing. Remember that insider trading has the most predictive value if it involves a substantial number of insiders and the number of shares traded is a substantial proportion of insiders' current holdings.

12

OPTIONS ON STOCKS

Trading volume in stock options has grown remarkably since the creation of the Chicago Board Options Exchange (CBOE) in 1973. In 1997, the daily average options volume was 1.41 million contracts. That daily average increased to 1.62 million contracts for 1998 and hit 2.02 million in 1999, a more than 40% jump in two years. The listed option has become a practical investment vehicle for institutions and individuals seeking profit or protection. The CBOE is the world's largest options marketplace, with about half the share of the total options market. Options also are traded on the AMEX, the Pacific Exchange, and the Philadelphia Stock Exchange. The CBOE trades options on individual stocks, Standard & Poor's 100 and 500 market indexes, the Russell 2000 Index, the Nasdaq-100 Index, the DJIA, the Internet Commerce Index, and others.

What Are Options? An option is a contract that provides a holder (buyer) the right to purchase from or sell to the issuer (writer) a specified interest at a designated price called the strike price (exercise price) for a given period of time. Therefore, three conditions are specified in options contracts:

1. The property to be delivered
2. The price of the property
3. A specified time period during which the right held by the buyer can be exercised

Options have standardized terms including the strike price and the expiration time. This standardization makes it possible for buyers or writers of options to close out their positions by offsetting sales and purchases. By selling an option with the same terms as the one purchased, or buying an option with the same terms as the one sold, an investor can liquidate a position at any time.

Two types of options contracts exist: the *call option* and the *put option*. A call option gives the buyer the right to purchase a specified quantity of the underlying interest at a fixed price at any time during the life of the option. For example, an option to buy 100 shares of the common stock of XYZ Corporation at $50 until a specified day in September is an XYZ $50 September call. Alternatively, a put option gives the buyer the right to sell a specified quantity of the underlying interest at a fixed price at any time during the life of the option.

The last date on which the buyer is entitled to exercise an option is called the option exercise date. An option not exercised prior to expiration ceases to exist. Note in Exhibit 6 that there are prices for different months. All CBOE stock options expire on the Saturday following the third Friday of the expiration month.

An in-the-money option occurs when the strike price of a call option is lower than the market value of the stock *or* the strike price of a put option is higher than the market price of the stock. An out-of-the money option occurs when the strike price of a call option is higher than the market price of a stock *or* the strike price of the put option is lower than the market value of the stock. An out-of-the money option will have little, if any, value just before the expiration date. However, an in-the-money option has financial value, and the investor must exercise or sell the option before it expires and becomes worthless.

Intrinsic and Time Value. The value of an option is often viewed as consisting of two components: intrinsic value and time value. Intrinsic value reflects the amount by which an option is in the money. For example, when the market price of XYZ stock is $56 per share, an XYZ $50 call has an intrinsic value of $6.

Time value reflects what the buyer is willing to pay for an option in anticipation of price changes prior to expiration. The time value of an option typically decreases as the option approaches expiration.

EXHIBIT 6
Listed Options Quotations

Option/Strike		Exp.	—Call— Vol.	—Call— Last	—Put— Vol.	—Put— Last
ACTV	50	Jan	210	$3\frac{1}{8}$	100	$7\frac{1}{2}$
AES Cp	65	Jan	…	…	210	$\frac{3}{4}$
$74\frac{3}{4}$	70	Feb	255	$8\frac{3}{4}$	…	…
ASM Intl	25	Feb	175	$1\frac{1}{16}$	…	…
AT&T	50	Jan	645	$2\frac{3}{8}$	705	$1\frac{7}{16}$
$50\frac{13}{16}$	50	Feb	102	$3\frac{3}{8}$	394	$2\frac{7}{16}$
$50\frac{13}{16}$	55	Jan	1229	$\frac{5}{8}$	129	$4\frac{3}{4}$
$50\frac{13}{16}$	55	Feb	196	$1\frac{7}{16}$	18	$5\frac{1}{2}$
$50\frac{13}{16}$	60	Jan	631	$\frac{1}{8}$	87	$9\frac{7}{8}$
$50\frac{13}{16}$	60	Feb	465	$\frac{9}{16}$	75	10
AberFitch	20	Jan	250	$6\frac{3}{4}$	…	…
$26\frac{11}{16}$	$32\frac{1}{2}$	Feb	200	$1\frac{1}{4}$	…	…
$26\frac{11}{16}$	35	Feb	240	$\frac{5}{8}$	2	$8\frac{3}{8}$
A M D	25	Jan	3770	$5\frac{1}{8}$	26	$1\frac{1}{8}$
$28\frac{15}{16}$	$27\frac{1}{2}$	Jan	1546	$3\frac{1}{2}$	45	$1\frac{7}{8}$
$28\frac{15}{16}$	30	Jan	426	$2\frac{3}{16}$	51	$3\frac{1}{2}$
$28\frac{15}{16}$	35	Jan	167	$\frac{3}{4}$	…	…
AdvRdio	20	Feb	395	$4\frac{3}{4}$	…	…
$23\frac{13}{16}$	$22\frac{1}{2}$	Jan	194	$2\frac{15}{16}$	108	$1\frac{3}{8}$
$23\frac{13}{16}$	$22\frac{1}{2}$	Feb	420	4	…	…
Affymet	180	Jan	33	$17\frac{1}{4}$	200	25
Alcati	50	Jan	200	$\frac{11}{16}$	…	…
AllegTel	95	Jan	161	$5\frac{3}{4}$	…	…
Allste	25	Jan	57	$\frac{5}{8}$	405	$1\frac{1}{2}$
$24\frac{1}{16}$	25	Feb	163	$1\frac{5}{16}$	…	…
Altera	55	Jan	182	$1\frac{7}{16}$	…	…
$49\frac{1}{16}$	65	Jan	163	$\frac{5}{16}$	…	…
AlterraHl	5	May	…	…	250	$\frac{3}{4}$
Alza	30	Jan	545	5	…	…
Amazon	60	Jan	113	$18\frac{7}{8}$	321	$1\frac{11}{16}$
76	65	Jan	35	14	260	$2\frac{7}{8}$
76	$67\frac{1}{2}$	Jan	2	$14\frac{1}{8}$	2020	$4\frac{1}{8}$
76	70	Jan	137	$10\frac{3}{8}$	379	$4\frac{3}{4}$
76	70	Feb	121	16	192	$8\frac{3}{4}$
76	75	Jan	122	9	293	$6\frac{3}{4}$
76	$77\frac{1}{2}$	Jan	283	$7\frac{1}{8}$	230	$7\frac{3}{4}$
76	80	Jan	1722	$6\frac{1}{8}$	970	$9\frac{1}{2}$
76	80	Feb	1112	11	161	$13\frac{3}{8}$
76	85	Jan	657	$4\frac{7}{8}$	3112	$12\frac{3}{4}$
76	90	Jan	424	$3\frac{3}{4}$	571	$16\frac{7}{8}$
76	90	Feb	276	$7\frac{3}{4}$	15	21
76	95	Jan	3185	$2\frac{9}{16}$	86	$20\frac{3}{8}$
76	100	Jan	936	2	45	$24\frac{3}{4}$
76	100	Feb	163	$5\frac{5}{8}$	10	$27\frac{7}{8}$
76	105	Jan	380	$1\frac{1}{2}$	112	$29\frac{1}{4}$
76	105	Feb	165	$4\frac{5}{8}$	10	$31\frac{1}{8}$
76	110	Jan	343	$1\frac{1}{16}$	69	$34\frac{1}{8}$
76	110	Apr	168	$7\frac{5}{8}$	…	…
76	115	Jan	157	$\frac{3}{4}$	…	…
76	120	Jan	452	$\frac{7}{8}$	…	…

38

Options Versus Stock. Options traded on exchanges such as the CBOE are similar in many respects to securities traded on other exchanges:

1. Options are listed securities.
2. Orders to trade options are conducted through brokers in the same manner as orders to buy and sell stock. Similarly to stock, orders on listed options are executed on the trading floor of a national exchange where trading is conducted in an auction market.
3. The price, volume, and other information about options is almost instantly available, as it is for stock.

These differences between stock and options should be recognized:

1. Unlike shares of common stock, there is no fixed number of options. The number of options depends upon the number of buyers and sellers.
2. Unlike stock, there are no certificates as evidence of ownership. Ownership of options is indicated by printed statements prepared by the involved brokerage firms.
3. An option is a wasting asset. An option that is not sold or exercised prior to expiration becomes worthless, and the holder loses the full purchase price.

Who Should Buy Options? Options have some definite advantages. First, the maximum loss is limited to the premium paid for the option. Second, options can produce quick profits with little capital. Third, options are flexible and can be combined with other investments to protect positions and profits.

However, only investors with well-defined investment objectives and a plan for realizing these objectives should trade in options. Successful options traders must thoroughly research options, understand options strategies, and closely follow the options market on a day-to-day basis. Explanatory materials on options trading are available from the CBOE web site at *www.cboe.com.*

13

INTERNATIONAL INVESTMENTS

As the world economy becomes increasingly interdependent, many investors are now realizing that profits can be made by investing in foreign securities. With about half of the world's publicly traded stocks registered outside the United States, opportunities abound for the investor willing to expend the time and effort in analyzing these foreign markets. Do not be misled by the Asian market's meltdown in 1997, or the dismal performance of the Japanese market in the 1990s as compared to the United States. Although the U.S. market strongly outperformed foreign markets over most of the 1990s, this record was not typical. Over 24 years from 1969 to 1993, the Morgan Stanley Capital International Index, which reflects all major markets outside North America, gained 904%, more than threefold the 277% increase of the U.S. market.

Investing in international stocks is an excellent way to diversify a stock portfolio. In *A Random Walk Down Wall Street* (W.W. Norton & Company, 1999), Burton Malkiel writes that over a 21-year period from 1977 to 1997, the mix of stocks that provided the highest return available with the least risk was 24% in the developed foreign country stocks (Europe, Australia, and Far East) and 76% in U.S. stocks.

An investment in a foreign stock can lead to a profit or loss in two ways:

1. The price of the stock in its local currency can advance or decline.
2. Relative to the U.S. dollar, the value of the foreign currency may rise or fall.

Of the several different methods for investing in foreign stock, the three most popular for individual investors are (1) American depositary receipts (ADRs), (2) mutual funds, and (3) iShares (see Key 31).

American Depositary Receipts (ADRs). Individuals who wish to purchase specific foreign securities should purchase ADRs. ADRs are negotiable receipts representing ownership of stock in a foreign corporation traded on an exchange. ADRs are only issued on widely held and actively traded corporations. Furthermore, they are liquid and have transaction costs comparable to U.S. stock. They are issued by an American bank and represent shares on deposit with the American bank's foreign office or custodian. ADRs allow investors to buy or sell foreign securities without actually taking physical possession of these securities. Purchase is made, and dividends are received, in U.S. dollars. Approximately 600 foreign corporations have ADRs listed against their securities, with the great majority traded in the over-the-counter market. In 1999, the Bank of New York's ADR index rose 46%, more than double the increase of the S&P 500. An excellent web site for information and prices is *www.worldlyinvestor.com.*

Mutual Funds. The easiest way to invest in foreign securities is to buy shares in one of the mutual funds that confines its investments to foreign securities. This course of action is preferable for those investors who lack the time or inclination to investigate these foreign markets closely. International stock funds offer the advantage of participation in a diversified portfolio of foreign stock, as well as professional management. International funds are now available that specialize in particular regions, such as Asia, or specific countries, such as Brazil or Germany. Prior to purchasing any of these funds the investor should obtain a copy of the prospectus. A prospectus will describe the investment philosophy of the fund. (See Key 27 for a more detailed explanation of mutual funds.)

14

GROSS DOMESTIC PRODUCT

Gross Domestic Product (GDP) represents the total market value of the final output of goods and services produced within the boundaries of the United States, whether by American or foreign-supplied resources. The GDP is the broadest single measure of U.S. economic activity and is usually considered to be the best available indicator of the economy's health. As a result, it receives strong media interest. The GDP reports are percentage changes reported as an annual rate. For example, on November 24, 1999, the change in GDP was estimated as an annual growth rate of 5.5% in the third quarter, pushing the nation's total output of goods and services to an annual rate of $8.9 trillion, after adjusting for inflation.

GDP is a quarterly figure but it is released on a monthly basis, generally between the twenty-sixth and thirty-first day of the month. The first estimate for a particular quarter—referred to as the advance estimate—is issued by the Commerce Department during the fourth week of the first month following the reference quarter. For example, the first-quarter advance estimate is published in late April and subsequent first estimates are released in July, October, and January. The second estimate, called the preliminary estimate, is released a month later and the third or final estimate is issued in the third month of the succeeding quarter. Annual revisions are released in July for the previous three years plus the quarters already published in the current year. Finally, benchmark revisions occur about every five years to include information from the periodic surveys the government conducts of the economy. This information is reported on the Commerce Department web site, *www.doc.gov.*

Included in the GDP reports is an index of prices paid for gross domestic purchases, which is the broadest measure and best reflects the movement of prices in a dynamic economy. This measure of inflation is usually lower than the consumer price index (see Key 16) because it captures consumers' ability to substitute less-expensive alternatives in response to price increases.

Finally, stock market participants should be aware that preliminary estimates of GNP tend to be more newsworthy than revised estimates to the financial markets. The average revision from the advanced report to the final is about 0.5 percentage point.

The measurement of GDP involves productive transactions only—the final purchase of newly produced goods or services. Excluded are nonproductive transactions, which can be broken down into two categories: financial transactions, such as the buying and selling of securities, government transfer payments (e.g., Social Security), and private transfer payments (gifts); and the transfer of used goods.

GDP can be broken down into four components:

1. Personal consumption expenditures
2. Government expenditures
3. Gross private domestic investment
4. Net exports

Personal consumption expenditures include expenditures by households on consumer goods and services. *Government expenditures* include federal, state, and local governmental spending on the finished products of businesses plus all direct purchases of resources by government. *Gross private domestic investment* refers to investment spending by business firms in future productive capacity, including changes in inventory.

GDP is also increased by *net exports*: the production

of goods and services that are exported decreased by the total value of imported goods, which do not reflect productive activity in the U.S. economy. If the value of the exports is less than the value of the imports, the figure is negative, reducing the GDP.

These four components add up to GDP. The equation that represents this relationship is

$$GDP = C + I + G + NE$$

where   C = consumption expenditures,
I = investment expenditures,
G = government expenditures,
NE = total exports minus total imports.

Adjusting Gross Domestic Product. Because of the effects of inflation, comparisons of GDP for different years using the reported numbers can be misleading. GDP can be adjusted by expressing it in terms of real purchasing power using a particular year as a standard of comparison. When GDP is corrected for changes in price, it is called real GDP. If GDP is expressed in current dollars without adjusting for price changes, it is referred to as nominal GDP.

A more meaningful measure of economic well-being for many purposes is to compute GDP on a per capita basis. For example, if real GDP had increased by 15% over a ten-year period during which the population had increased by 25%, the nation's citizens would be less well off than previously. To adjust for changes in population, real GDP can be divided by population to obtain per capita real GDP.

Deficiencies of Gross Domestic Product. Although GDP is designed to measure the total value of all goods and services produced in the economy, certain activities are not included by government statisticians. Productive do-it-yourself activities are not included in GDP because these transactions are not reflected in the marketplace. Of even greater significance is the omission of services performed by individuals in the home. These services would be included if performed by a housekeeper. Finally, illegal activities such as narcotics dealing, gambling, and prostitution are not included in the calculation of GDP. Unreported activities may account for 10% to 20% of measured GDP, and they are growing faster than the reported activities. The greater the significance of the underground economy relative to total economic activity, the more the reported amount of GDP may be underestimating the true value of total output.

15

LEADING ECONOMIC INDICATORS

Around the first of each month, the Conference Board, a private nonprofit organization, publishes three indicators of business activity. The index that receives the most widespread media attention is the Index of Leading Economic Indicators. The other two indexes are the Index of Coincident Economic Indicators and the Index of Lagging Economic Indicators. These indicators are published in *Business Cycle Indicators*, a useful publication for anyone interested in evaluating economic activity. The indicators are listed in Exhibit 7.

The leading indicators are important because investors are more interested in the future path of the economy than they are in what is happening currently (coincident indicators) or what has happened (lagging indicators). The leading indicators are not completely reliable. In fact, more than one third of the time they give false signals. The leading indicators generally peak about five months before a recession, but this varies. The index peaked about eight months before the recessions of 1969–1970 and 1974, but only three months before the recession of 1981–1982, and six months before the recession of 1990. Overall, the index has been more successful at anticipating recoveries than in predicting recessions. Many economists believe that the index of leading indicators needs a major overhaul. They find it increasingly less relevant to the economy's actual performance or prospects. Geoffrey Moore, former head of the Center for International Business Cycle Research at Columbia University, has cited several deficiencies in the index that impair its usefulness. For example, the United States increasingly is becoming a part of the global economy, but the indexes primarily reflect domestic activity.

In addition, Moore laments the fact that the service sector, which is becoming increasingly important in the economy, is underrepresented. An examination of the ten leading indicators in Exhibit 7 shows that they primarily relate to the production and manufacture of goods.

How to Use the Index. The Index of Leading Economic Indicators can be thought of as a useful tool in predicting turning points. A rule of thumb is that three successive monthly declines, or increases, in the index indicate that the economy may soon turn in the same direction. Remember that monthly moves in the index are not as important as the cumulative long-run trend. Historically, the leading index has a shorter lead in predicting turning points leading to recovery than to downturns. Therefore, a strengthening index should lead to a relatively quick improvement in the economy. Additional information can be obtained at the Conference Board's web site at *www.conference-board.org*.

EXHIBIT 7
Economic Indicators

Leading Economic Indicators

1. Average weekly hours paid to production workers in manufacturing
2. Average weekly claims for unemployment insurance
3. New orders for consumer goods and materials
4. Index of 500 common stock prices
5. Manufacturers' new orders, nondefense capital goods
6. Index of building permits for new private housing units
7. Vendor performance—slower deliveries index
8. Money supply (M2)
9. Interest rate spread, ten-year Treasury bonds less federal funds
10. Index of consumer expectations

Coincident Economic Indicators

1. Employees on nonagricultural payrolls
2. Index of industrial production
3. Personal income minus transfer payments
4. Manufacturing, wholesale, and retail sales

Lagging Economic Indicators

1. Index of labor cost per unit of output in manufacturing
2. Ratio of manufacturing and trade inventory to sales
3. Average duration of unemployment
4. Ratio of consumer installment debt to personal income
5. Commercial and industrial loans outstanding
6. Average prime interest rate charged by banks
7. Change in consumer price index for services

16

INFLATION

One of the single most important determinants of the stunning 19% yearly increase in stock prices during the decade of the 1990s was the low rate of inflation. Inflation averaged a slim 1.9% in the 1990s, down from 5.1% in the 1980s and 7.4% in the 1970s. Although this record is commendable, the Federal Reserve realizes that continual vigilance is required to guard against the overheating of the economy. Between 1970 and 1999, the general level of prices as measured by the Consumer Price Index more than quadrupled. Inflation causes great concern because it results in the redistribution of wealth when it is not anticipated. For example, inflation tends to benefit borrowers at the expense of lenders whenever inflation rates are underestimated over the life of a loan. If $10,000 is borrowed for one year and the inflation rate for that year is 3%, the dollars of principal repaid at the end of the year have depreciated by 3%. The borrower benefits by repaying less real dollars, while the lender receives dollars whose purchasing power has declined. Hence, inflation causes the lender to lose.

Inflation can also have a corrosive effect on savings. As prices rise, the value of savings will decline if the rate of inflation exceeds the rate of interest. People on fixed incomes are hurt by inflation. The workers who retired in 1990 on a fixed pension found that by 1999 the purchasing power of their monthly check had declined by more than 25%.

The importance of low inflation to the financial markets was again emphasized when the Bureau of Labor Statistics (BLS) reported on May 14, 1999, that the Consumer Price Index jumped an unexpected 0.7% in

April. Worries over the threat of rising inflation caused the Dow Jones Industrial Average to tumble by 194 points and pushed the yield on long-term Treasury bonds to a 12-month high of 5.92%.

Measuring Inflation. If inflation is defined as a rise in the general level of prices, how is it measured? This problem is easily solved when referring to the price change of one good, but the solution becomes trickier when dealing with a large number of goods, some with prices that have risen faster than others. Realistically, price changes for all the goods produced by the economy cannot be computed. Instead, statisticians for the federal government select a representative market basket of goods and then compute the price changes of the market basket every month.

One way to gain an appreciation for the effect of inflation is to employ the "rule of 72." This method provides an approximate measure of the number of years required for the price level to double. The number 72 is divided by the annual rate of inflation:

$$\text{Number of years required} \atop \text{for prices to double} = \frac{72}{\text{Annual rate of inflation}}$$

For example, the price level will double in approximately 24 years if the inflation rate is 3% per year. Similarly, inflation of 5% per year means the price level will double in about 14 years. Savers can use this formula to estimate how long it will take their savings to double.

Prominent Price Indexes. Three price indexes calculated by government statisticians receive a great deal of attention in the financial press: the Consumer Price Index (CPI), the Producer Price Index (PPI), and the Gross Domestic Product (GDP) deflator. Each of these indexes measures the average price change for the goods and services that comprise the index. The changes in these indexes are highly correlated over time, and each reveals the persistence of inflation in recent economic history.

The Consumer Price Index. The CPI is the most widely cited index in the media. The CPI attempts to measure changes in the prices of goods and services purchased by urban consumers. The Bureau of Labor Statistics computes the index monthly based upon data collected in 91 cities on the price changes of approximately 400 goods and services in eight broad categories: education and communication, food, clothing, housing, transportation, medical care, entertainment, and other. The CPI is considered to be the most reliable measure of changes in the cost of living for most American families. Prices for 1982–1984 represent the base year for the CPI, which is set at 100. For example, the CPI measured in 1999 was almost 70% more than the level of 1982. This index is reported on about the twelfth business day of the month at *http://stats.bls.gov/news.release/cpi.toc.htm.*

Producer Price Index. The PPI, formerly called the Wholesale Price Index, measures changes in the average prices of goods received by producers of commodities, in all stages of processing, in primary or wholesale markets. The PPI measures the change in prices paid by businesses rather than by consumers. The market basket for calculating the PPI consists of about 3,200 items purchased by producers and manufacturers, including crude, intermediate, and finished goods (see Exhibit 8).

Because primary products included in the PPI are processed into finished goods distributed to retail markets, many analysts believe that changes in the PPI precede changes in the CPI. For this reason, the PPI is closely followed as a leading indicator of consumer prices. However, this relationship does not always hold true. Because the PPI does not include services, the price changes of CPI and PPI may not correlate when the price of services changes at a rate that is different from the rate for other price changes. This index is reported on about the tenth business day of the month at *http://stats.bls.gov/news.release/ppi.toc.htm.*

Gross Domestic Product Deflator. The GDP deflator

is the most broadly based of the price level indicators. The GDP includes price changes on not only goods and services that households purchase (about two thirds of GDP), but also expenditures by government, investment by business, and purchases by the foreign sector. Thus, the GDP deflator measures the prices of all final goods and services.

The GDP deflator is calculated as a by-product of the calculation of current and real GDP. This deflator is obtained by dividing current-year quantities at current-year prices by current-year quantities at base-year prices (the base year is currently 1992.) Unlike the CPI and the PPI, which are reported monthly, both the GDP and the GDP deflator are calculated and reported quarterly.

EXHIBIT 8
Example Reporting of the Producer Price Index
PRODUCER PRICES

Here is the Labor Department's Producer Price Index (1982 = 100) for November 1999, before seasonal adjustment, and the percentage changes from November 1998.

Finished goods	135.0	3.1%
Minus food & energy	147.4	1.8%
Intermediate goods	125.4	3.0%
Crude goods	108.6	16.0%

Source: *Wall Street Journal*

Over the years common stocks have been a better inflation hedge than bonds or Treasury securities. As a general proposition, lower inflation leads to higher returns for stocks and bonds, while higher inflation reduces returns on stocks and bonds. Bonds with longer-term maturities are particularly risky when inflation unexpectedly heats up. The Federal Reserve responds to the threat of inflation by raising interest rates, which pushes down the price of bonds. Physical goods or assets such as real estate, precious metals, art objects, and collectibles have been excellent inflation hedges. However, the declines in the prices of gold and silver in recent years show there are no guarantees that even real assets will continue to outstrip the rate of inflation.

Future Trends in Inflation. What should the investor look for in the news to appraise the future prospects of inflation? Three good indicators to watch are the capacity-utilization rate, unemployment rate (see Key 22), and the National Association of Purchasing Managers' Index.

Capacity utilization measures what manufacturers currently produce as compared with the most they could produce. This measure provides you with an excellent indication of whether the economy is operating near full capacity. Rising capacity utilization rates indicate increasing pressure on the economy's resource base. Higher utilization brings less efficient, higher cost capacity into production and is often accompanied by tighter labor markets that put further upward pressure on wages.

The Federal Reserve closely watches this indicator, and investors should also. When capacity utilization exceeds 85%, inflation becomes a threat to the economy. The Fed releases this indicator about the fifteenth day of the month on its web site, *www.bog.frb.fed.us*.

The National Association of Purchasing Managers' Index is a composite index measuring manufacturing activity. Readings above 60% often indicate that the economy is overheating. A reading below 44% signals a widespread contradiction in the economy. This index is reported at *www.napm.org* on the first business day of each month.

17

FEDERAL RESERVE SYSTEM

The Federal Reserve System is a complex organization that includes the Board of Governors of the Federal Reserve System, the Federal Open Market Committee, and the 12 regional Federal Reserve Banks. The Federal Reserve (Fed) is the central bank, and the Fed has many functions, as outlined below. Although the Fed does not control interest rates, it can significantly influence interest rates through control of the money supply. The Fed's importance in our financial system is pervasive, and knowledge of its purposes and functions is critical to investors.

Structure of the Fed. At the top of the Federal Reserve's organization structure is the Board of Governors. The primary function of the Board is the formulation of monetary policy; in addition, the Board has broad responsibilities for the activities of national and state-chartered member banks. The seven members of the Board are appointed by the president and confirmed by the Senate. All appointments are for 14-year terms, theoretically insulating the Board from short-term political influence. The president also designates the chairman and the vice chairman, who serve for four-year terms with redesignation possible as long as their terms as Board members have not expired. The chairman of the Board occupies a powerful position, often cited as being second only to that of the president.

Implementation of Monetary Policy. The most important responsibility of the Fed is the control of the money supply. The three principal tools the Fed can use to regulate the money supply are as follows:

1. *Open market operations*: The most important policy instrument of the Fed involves buying and selling U.S. government securities in the open market. Decisions are made by the Federal Open Market Committee, consisting of the seven members of the Board of Governors, the president of the Federal Reserve Bank of New York, and four other presidents of reserve banks. The financial community closely monitors these activities. Banks are required to maintain cash reserves against the money they loan. The larger a bank's reserves, the more money it is able to loan, and the more money a bank is able to lend, the larger the money supply tends to be. When the Fed purchases securities (e.g., Treasury bills), and the seller is an individual or nonbank corporation, the seller generally deposits the check in a commercial bank, which presents it to the Fed for credit. This event increases the reserves of the bank, permitting it to increase the money available to lend.

   Conversely, when the Fed sells securities, the opposite occurs. A nonbank buyer pays the Fed with a check drawn on a bank. The Fed deducts this check from the bank's reserve balance, and the bank has less money to lend, restricting growth in the money supply. Thus, the purchase of securities raises bank reserves, while Fed sales of securities lower reserves. The effect is immediate and the adjustment of reserves is precise. The Fed employs this method daily as needed.

2. *Discount window*: The discount window is the place in the Federal Reserve System where banks go to borrow money. Discounting occurs when the Fed lends reserves to member banks. The rate of interest the Fed charges is called the discount rate. The rate is altered periodically as market conditions change or to complement open market operations. The rate is primarily of interest as an indi-

cation of the Federal Reserve's view of the economy and money and credit demand.

3. *Reserve requirements*: Banks are required to maintain reserves against the money they loan. When reserve requirements are increased, the amount of deposits supported by the supply of reserves is reduced, and banks have to reduce their loans. Although powerful, this tool is less flexible than the other two policy instruments and, therefore, is seldom used.

Effect of Fed Action. In 1999, the Federal Reserve, concerned about signs that inflationary pressures were building, hiked interest rates three times. By July 2000, the Fed had hiked interest rates three more times. These actions indicated the Fed's resolve to dampen inflationary expectations that might result from an overheated economy and an ebullient stock market. Rising interest rates heighten investors' concern because the higher the interest debt that securities pay, the more attractive they become to investors as compared to stocks, thereby encouraging the flow of funds from stocks to bonds. In addition, the higher rates increase debt costs for businesses, an expense that reduces net income. Companies that are highly leveraged, such as banks, are particularly vulnerable.

The investment adviser Edson Gould formalized this concern about 50 years ago when he developed a trading rule called "three steps and a stumble." As he stated, three consecutive tightening moves by the Fed signal a coming downturn in stock prices. Though widely publicized in the media, Gould's rule does not hold up to analysis. In the last 55 years, interest rates have been raised three times in a row on nine occasions. Although each time the market fell, on seven of those occasions stock prices were up six months later.

More critical to the course of the market is investors' confidence that the Fed will be able to contain inflation without bringing on a damaging recession. The Fed continually faces a delicate balancing act, for if rates are raised too much, corporate profits and economic activity will suffer, and if the Fed fails to act strongly enough, rising inflation will result. The Fed's activities can be followed at *www.bog.frb.fed.us*.

18

MONEY SUPPLY

The definition of the money supply causes economists continuing problems. The Federal Reserve has
periodically redefined its definitions of money because
of the emergence of new types of financial instruments
such as negotiable orders of withdrawal (NOW) accounts,
repurchase agreements (RPs or REPOs), and money
market deposit accounts (MMDAs). Currently, the Fed
has subdivided the money supply into four categories:
M1, M2, M3, and L.

M1 is currency in circulation plus all checking accounts,
including those that pay interest, such as NOW accounts.
M1 is the narrowest definition of the money supply and
represents money primarily held to carry out transactions.
Over 65% of M1 represents demand deposits, while less
than 35% consists of currency and coin.

M2 expands M1 to include items that are not quite as
liquid, including

1. Certain short-term deposits at Caribbean branches
   of member banks held by U.S. nonbank residents
2. Money market mutual fund (MMMF) balances
3. Money market deposit accounts (MMDAs)
4. Savings and small-denomination time deposits
   (e.g., CDs) of less than $100,000

M3 is the broadest measure of the money supply,
adding to M2 other liquid assets that are owned predom-
inantly by wealthy individuals and institutions. Examples
include

1. RPs or REPOs, which are agreements made by banks
   to sell government securities to customers and,

simultaneously, to repurchase the same securities at a price that includes accumulated interest. RPs offer a way to earn interest on idle cash.

2. Time deposits and certain other instruments through which funds are loaned in large denominations ($100,000 or more) to depository institutions
3. Eurodollars held by U.S. residents
4. Shares in money market funds that are generally restricted to institutions

The Fed also publishes a broader measure of liquidity, called L. This measure includes a variety of short-term market instruments. Examples are

1. Banker's acceptances
2. Commercial paper
3. Marketable Treasury and agency obligations with original maturities of less than 12 months

This measure is not used as a target for monetary policy because data on it are not promptly available.

Significance of the Money Supply. The supply of money is of crucial importance to economic activity. The money supply is one of the most useful leading indicators (see Key 15). In addition, money supply is also used by many analysts for insight into the future course of stock prices. Changes in the total money supply and the rate at which it increases or decreases affect important economic variables such as the inflation rate, interest rate, employment, and gross domestic product. The control of the money supply is the primary responsibility of the Fed (see Key 17). An increase in the money supply relative to demand for it causes interest rates to fall, stimulating investment spending, output, and employment. The converse is also true.

Particularly when resources are fully employed, an increasing money supply has inflationary consequences. When more money exists than is needed to carry out transactions, inflation will result. However, inflation does not immediately follow an acceleration in money growth. This inflationary process has historically taken from one and one half to two years, although in recent years changes in the money supply have been a less reliable indicator of future inflation. Monetary indicators may have become less reliable in predicting future inflation because of the introduction of new financial instruments such as NOW accounts, RPs, and MMDAs. In addition, some economists blame their poor record on problems in the banking system. Now that banks are healthy, the money supply may once again become a valid indicator.

Reporting the Ms. The money supply numbers are reported every Thursday afternoon. Fed watchers analyze these numbers for clues to the direction of monetary policy. Although M1 receives the greatest attention in the media, M2 is more closely watched by most economists. M2 is also the money supply number included in the leading economic indicators. The Federal Reserve Board web site is at *www.bog.frb.fed.us.*

19

INTEREST RATES

The interest rate is the price a borrower pays for the use of a lender's money. Interest is usually expressed as an annual rate or percentage rather than as an absolute amount. Thus, if an individual borrows $100 for one year, a payment of $10 on the amount borrowed translates to 10% annual simple interest. Interest rates are usually set by market forces and vary greatly in differing circumstances. A loan to buy a house may cost the borrower 6% to 9% annual interest. Department store and bank charge cards often charge 18% to 20% annual interest. However, the federal government usually pays 4% to 8% interest on its debt. Variations in the interest paid result from many factors, including length of loans, risk to the lender, and administrative costs.

EXHIBIT 9
Key Rates

Percent

	Yesterday	Day Ago	Year Ago
Prime rate	**8.50**	8.50	8.50
Discount rate	**5.00**	5.00	5.00
Federal funds	**3.50**	4.86	4.80
3-month T-bills	**5.05**	5.23	4.42
6-month T-bills	**5.40**	5.45	4.42
10-yr. T-infl.	**4.32**	4.32	3.85
10-yr. T-note	**6.38**	6.42	4.64
30-yr. T-bond	**6.44**	6.47	5.08
Telephone bd.	**8.30**	8.44	6.75
Municipal bds.	**6.22**	6.22	5.16

Sources: Salomon Smith Barney; Telerate; *The Bond Buyer*

Real Versus Nominal Interest Rates. The nominal

interest rate is the rate of interest expressed in current dollars. Inflation causes the nominal interest rate to be higher, as the rate rises to reflect the anticipated rate of inflation. The real interest rate is obtained by subtracting the anticipated rate of inflation from the nominal rate of interest. If the nominal rate of interest is 3% and the rate of inflation is 3%, the real rate of interest is zero.

Panoply of Interest Rates. Although all interest rates tend to move in the same direction at the same time, an examination of the financial pages reveals that there are dozens of different interest rates (see Exhibit 9). Some of the most widely quoted interest rates are as follows:

1. Federal funds rate is the rate banks have to pay to borrow reserves from other banks. A rise in the federal funds rate indicates that more banks are running short of reserves, whereas a fall indicates the opposite. This rate also provides an indication of Federal Reserve monetary policy. A rising trend in the rate signals a more restrictive policy, whereas a fall indicates a more expansionary policy. However, sharp fluctuations can occur from one day to the next without signaling a change in policy.

2. Prime rate is the rate charged by commercial banks to their most creditworthy business customers. Businesses that are less creditworthy are charged a higher interest rate.

3. Commercial paper is the rate on short-term, unsecured (i.e., no collateral) debt issued by large corporations and other borrowers to investors with surplus cash. The interest rate is usually less than that charged by banks.

4. Mortgage rate is the rate charged by thrift institutions to home buyers. Up to 90% of the cost of a home is usually borrowed and repaid in monthly installments over 15 to 30 years. A climb in mortgage rates raises monthly payments and has a depressing effect on new home construction.

5. Treasury bill rate is the rate on short-term securi-

ties that mature in 13 weeks, 26 weeks, or 52 weeks and are issued in minimum denominations of $1,000 and larger amounts in multiples of $1,000 face amount. Treasury bills are sold at a discount from face value and are redeemed at full face value upon maturity. Since they are guaranteed by the full faith and credit of the U.S. government, they are the safest of securities.

6. Treasury note rate is the rate on Treasury securities that mature in from two to ten years. Mortgage rates closely track the 10-year Treasury note.

7. Bond rates depend upon the length of the bond term and the creditworthiness of the issuer. Generally speaking, bonds that mature in 30 years pay a higher rate than bonds maturing in 10 years. The reason is that price fluctuates with changes in the level of interest rates, increasing the risk of capital loss over the longer term. Treasury bonds pay less interest than corporate bonds because, like Treasury bills and notes, they are guaranteed by the full faith and credit of the U.S. government. Treasury bonds mature in 30 years and are issued in $1,000 minimum denominations; $5,000, $10,000, $50,000, $100,000, and $1 million denominations also are available.

Yield Curve. The yield curve results from a graph that plots the relationship between the interest rates on short-term and long-term bonds. Thus, this curve shows in graphic form the relationship between maturity and a security's yield at a point in time. The resulting curve reveals whether short-term interest rates are higher or lower than long-term rates (see Exhibit 10).

As a rule, the yield curve slopes upward because interest rates usually rise with the length of the investment. The logic is simple: if investors commit their money for more time, they take more risk and demand a greater return. In unusual situations, when short-term Treasury securities yield higher rates than long-term bonds, there is an inverted yield curve (one that slopes downward).

EXHIBIT 10
Treasury Yield Curve
Yields as of 4:30 P.M. Eastern time

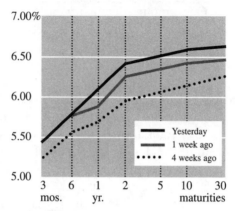

Source: Thomson Global Markets

The yield curve generally inverts when the Fed raises interest rates to slow down the economy and control inflation. The market sees the Fed fighting inflation, and this action reduces inflationary expectations, dampening the rate on long-term bonds. Typically, an inverted yield curve indicates that the market expects interest rates to decline in the future, accompanied by an economic contraction. What are the signs that interest rates are going to decline? Watch the trend in the federal funds rate. By setting the rate, the Fed effectively determines all short-term interest rates.

The link between the money markets and long-term interest rates is more tenuous. Long-term interest rates are primarily affected by inflationary expectations. Therefore, changes in short-term rates may not always correspond to changes in long-term rates. However, the Fed's clout should not be underestimated. If the Fed is aggressively easing or tightening credit, long-term rates will move in the same direction as short-term rates.

20

FISCAL POLICY

Fiscal policy refers to the federal government's policy in regard to taxation and spending. Fiscal policy is often differentiated from monetary policy, which refers to the actions of the Federal Reserve.

Discretionary fiscal policy is defined as a deliberate change in the rate of taxation or government spending by the federal government for the purpose of lowering unemployment or inflation. The federal government has the option of increasing or reducing governmental expenditures, raising or lowering taxes, or using a combination of the two to stabilize the economy. An expansionary fiscal policy should be employed when a recession occurs. Such a policy involves increasing government spending, or lowering taxes, or a combination of the two.

If inflation is a concern, a contractionary fiscal policy should be implemented. Such a policy consists of decreasing government spending, or raising taxes, or a combination of the two. Ideally, the federal government should attempt to achieve a budget surplus when the unemployment rate is low and the economy is faced with the problem of runaway inflation.

Supply-Side Economics. At least in the first years of the Reagan administration, supply-side economics had great influence over policy makers. The underlying assumption of supply-side economics is that individuals, in their capacities as workers, savers, and investors, will respond to changes in marginal tax rates. The higher the marginal tax rate, the greater the incentive to avoid paying taxes, either through legal tax avoidance, illegal tax evasion, or less work, saving, and investment. Alternatively, a reduction in marginal tax rates should actually increase tax revenues. This reasoning was behind the tax cut of 1981.

Since supply-siders did not believe that, aside from taxes, fiscal policy was very important, they did not cut planned government spending as much as tax revenues. Thus, government expenditures continued to rise as a percentage of GDP even though tax revenues stabilized. This rise in government expenditures increased the federal deficit dramatically.

To cut taxes without cutting total government expenditures at the same time is a mistake. Nevertheless, except for the large deficits, supply-side policies were not unsuccessful. In response to tax incentives, investment spending rose rapidly after 1982, and the economy continued to generate a large number of new jobs while prices rose slowly.

Monetary Policy Versus Fiscal Policy. Fiscal policy does not seem to work as advertised. Empirical testing has not found any correlation between the surplus or deficit and current or future economic activity. Increases in deficits have been followed by several recessions, and huge deficits have been accompanied by substantial unemployment, violating the theory of fiscal policy. A school of thought called monetarism asserts that changes in the supply of money are the determinants of economic activity. Monetarists focus upon the Fed as the most important player in determining the future course of the economy. They argue that fiscal policy is impotent in affecting future levels of economic activity. Although the debate about the importance of monetary policy versus fiscal policy continues, monetarists clearly have impressed upon the financial community the importance of the Fed's control over the money supply.

When monetary policy is eased, interest rates fall, bond prices rise, and stocks become more attractive because investors expect faster economic growth and higher corporate profits. Conversely, rising interest rates reduce bond prices and eventually slow economic growth and reduce corporate profits. Stock investors should remember that in the years since 1960, when inflation has been 4% or less, total real returns (returns adjusted for inflation) have averaged more than 14% annually. However, when inflation ranges from 4% to 7%, the average real rate of return on stocks has dropped to less than 3%.

21

MEASURES OF PRODUCTIVITY

Productivity measures are measures of efficiency in the use of resources. Productivity is defined as the average physical output produced per unit of input in any given time period. The greater the output produced from a given amount of inputs, the more productive is the economy. The key measure of productivity for the economy is labor productivity, which is defined as the ratio of real output to labor input measured in hours paid. In equation form,

$$\text{Labor productivity} = \frac{\text{Output}}{\text{Hours paid}} = \frac{\text{Average output}}{\text{Per hour}}$$

The importance of this ratio cannot be overstated. This measure is the most important indicator of the nation's efficiency. Real income and the standard of living of the population cannot increase without an increase in the productivity of the labor force.

In simple terms, productivity is the measure of what a worker can produce while working for one hour. However, the statement that high productivity indicates an enthusiastic, energetic labor force and low productivity implies a lazy labor force is generally not correct. Better indicators of the productivity of the labor force are the efficiency of the equipment the workers operate and their training and education. In recent years, the growth in productivity has been enhanced by advances in information technology and the Internet revolution.

Inflation and Productivity. One of the key factors in determining the level of inflation is the relationship between labor costs and productivity. Unit labor costs are equal to hourly compensation divided by output per unit of labor. There is a close relationship between increases in prices and increases in unit labor costs because increases in prices must equal the growth in unit labor costs and unit profits. Wage increases unaccompanied by similar increases in productivity foster inflation. Productivity permits profits to rise and wages to climb without accompanying inflation. Stagnating productivity means that higher wages are translated into rising unit labor costs.

The Productivity Slowdown. From 1948 to 1973, growth of output per worker was 2.45%. From 1973 to 1982, this growth had declined to about half the rate of the previous 25 years. The slackening of U.S. productivity growth has had a dampening effect on the improvement in living standards. Why did productivity grow so little after 1973? Although economists still debate the issue, several reasons are offered.

1. The tremendous technological lead after World War II was largely dissipated by the 1970s. This process was largely inevitable as other countries recovered from the destructive effects of World War II.
2. An erosion of business profits occurred because of the slowdown in economic growth and an increase in the rate of inflation. The decline in profit rates reduced the incentive to invest as evidenced by the reduction in the growth rate of capital stock.
3. A large number of young employees and married women entered the labor force with little or no previous work experience. Their relative lack of experience also meant that they were relatively less productive.

New Economy. The United States has seen the advent of what is called the new economy over the past several years. The new economy (see Key 26) is characterized by increases in productivity growth, a robust economy, and subdued inflation. Certainly, the end of the cold war, which freed up resources by moderating defense spending, the opening up of new global markets, Japan's slump, and the Asian meltdown in 1997–1998 have all been influential in holding down prices. But what may even be more significant in the long run are the advances in information technology and the stimulus of the Internet, which are generating increased competition and long-term efficiencies.

In 1999, the Commerce Department released results of a comprehensive revision of historical data on productivity. The biggest factor in the Commerce Department's revisions is the new way of accounting for software. The government now treats software purchases by business and government as investments, which are part of GDP. Previously, software spending was considered an expense, and expenses are not included in GDP. The government now recognizes that software is an investment, like machinery, which has a useful life of more than a year.

The revised data are illuminating. The beginning of the acceleration in productivity seems to coincide with the 1982 start of the long bull market in common stocks. Productivity growth in Reagan's administration (1981–1989) was 1.6%, significantly faster than Carter's 0.6%. In 1990–1998, productivity growth continued to advance to 2% with the rate accelerating in 1996–1998 to 2.6% and 3% in 1999.

If productivity growth continues to increase, economic growth could be sustained at high rates without the threat of inflation. Higher productivity spurs corporate profits while containing labor costs, which account for about two thirds of all business expenses. The year 1999 marked the fourth consecutive year that productivity had grown more than 2%, almost as good as 1961 to 1966. If this rate of growth is on a permanently higher plateau, the next decade could be an extremely prosperous one. This statistic is provided about six weeks after each quarter at *http://stats.bls.gov*.

22

UNEMPLOYMENT STATISTICS

Unemployment can be divided into three basic types: frictional, structural, and cyclical. *Frictional unemployment* is short-term unemployment that results from such factors as individuals voluntary switching jobs, fired employees seeking reemployment, employees seeking their first job, and the seasonal pattern of employment in such industries as construction and recreation.

Structural unemployment refers to long-term unemployment caused by changes in consumer demand and changes in technology. These types of changes cause some workers to become unemployed for long periods of time or permanently. Because of changes in the nature of the economy, the talents of some workers become obsolete. Structural unemployment is not caused by general business fluctuations, nor does it involve the normal movement of workers from one job to another.

Cyclical unemployment refers to unemployment caused by business fluctuations. This situation occurs when the economy is in a recession or depression and aggregate demand is insufficient to maintain full employment. When the overall level of business activity decreases, cyclical unemployment increases. Conversely, when overall business activity picks up, cyclical unemployment drops. A prominent economist, Arthur Okun, quantified the relationship between unemployment and GDP. This relationship, called Okun's law, indicates that the rate of unemployment declines by one percentage point for every two percentage points of increase in the rate of economic growth (GDP).

Full employment does not mean zero unemployment. Frictional and structural unemployment are unavoidable; thus the definition of full employment allows for less than 100% employment. One way to explain full employment is to say that it is achieved when cyclical unemployment is zero. But any definition of full employment is going to change as the demographics of the labor force change, institutional factors change, and the economy evolves.

Employment Report. The employment report is the single most important data series released by the government to both the bond and stock markets because it is both timely and a comprehensive measure of economic activity. Included in the report is the unemployment rate, which is determined by the Bureau of Labor Statistics by conducting a nationwide random survey of 60,000 households per month. The employment report is released on the first Friday of the month at *http://stats.bls.gov.*

Although the unemployment rate is the most widely reported statistic, this rate is a lagging indicator of the state of the economy. Instead, the market focuses upon the change in nonfarm payrolls, hours worked, and hourly pay. These numbers help predict whether the economy is strengthening or weakening, and if labor costs are accelerating or moderating.

The payroll survey collects data on jobs, hourly wages, and the number of hours in the workweek from about 400,000 companies covering nearly 50 industries. The total change in payrolls reflects economic activity. A big jump means companies are hiring in response to rising sales. A drop implies that companies are reducing their labor force in response to weakening sales.

In the recent past, the economic consensus was that at unemployment levels of less than about 6%, inflation was bound to accelerate. Yet joblessness had been 5% or less for 32 straight months by the end of 1999, and inflation had declined steadily through the 1990s, hitting a 12-year low in 1998. The Fed has expressed its concern about tight labor markets by raising interest rates three times in 1999 and again in February, March, and May of 2000. Although advances in information technology and the expanded use of the Internet may continue to stimulate efficiencies and lower costs, productivity growth must continue to increase rapidly to prevent unit labor costs from accelerating and heightening fears of inflation.

23

RETAIL SALES

The retail sales series is the most closely followed indicator for judging the strength of consumer spending. Watching consumer spending is critical to evaluating the strength of the economy because consumer spending accounts for about two thirds of gross domestic product. Therefore, the monthly retail sales report produced by the Census Bureau of the Commerce Department is of critical importance to the financial markets. Find the released report at *www.census.gov/cgi-bin/briefroom/briefrm.*

Retail sales data are released each month with the initial release called Advance Monthly Retail Sales. This report is released about nine business days after the end of every month and contains sales data for the previous month. The advance data is the market's first look at the strength of consumer demand.

Typically, the stock and bond markets have different hopes for the retail numbers. The bond market prefers sluggish retail sales because that indicates a slower overall economy. The stock market reaction is more complicated. Generally, strong retail sales are positive for stocks because that signals healthy economic activity. But, if the stock market is concerned about an overheated economy, strong retail sales could be bad news.

About 4,000 firms are surveyed to prepare the advance estimates. In the following month, the number will be revised to provide more complete as well as more accurate sales data by sampling an additional 10,000 retail businesses. The retail firms with the largest impact on sales are included in both surveys, reducing the impact of the larger sample on revisions of the data. A survey of about 22,000 retail establishments is conducted each year to provide annual revisions to retail sales.

Interpreting this data can be tricky. For example, retail sales data are grouped by kind of business rather than by type of goods sold. If you buy a nasal spray from Kroger's, it shows up under food rather than under drugs. In addition, sales of auto dealers comprise more than 20% of the total, and auto sales are extremely volatile. Fortunately, the Census Bureau publishes a nonauto retail number, which is a better indicator of the trend in consumer spending. Besides auto dealers, the two other largest groups are food (primarily grocery stores) and general merchandise (department stores and variety stores). Web retailers (although increasing in importance) still account for less than 1% of the $3 trillion in annual retail sales.

Policy makers consider retail sales data to be critical in evaluating the health of the economy. The retail sales numbers eventually become part of the monthly consumer spending report as well as the quarterly GDP calculation. Therefore, retail sales figures are an early warning signal on the health of the economy. The importance of retail sales was illustrated on December 15, 1999, when it was disclosed that retail sales jumped 0.9% in November compared with analysts' expectations of a 0.5% gain for the month. The strong showing raised concern on Wall Street that the Federal Reserve would raise short-term rates in the months ahead. Bond prices, which move in the opposite direction of interest rates, suffered a severe drop, and stock prices also fell.

24

CONSUMER CONFIDENCE SURVEYS

Consumer spending constitutes about two thirds of GDP. Because the consumer sector is so important, measurement of consumer confidence is critical to evaluating the trend of economic activity. People who are optimistic about the future are more likely to increase their spending. Two private institutions conduct monthly surveys of consumer confidence: (1) the Conference Board and (2) the University of Michigan Survey Research Center.

Both surveys ask consumers about their current attitudes regarding the economy as well as their outlook for 6 to 12 months in the future. In addition, consumers are asked if they intend to invest in housing or buy major items such as cars and appliances. Over the longer term, these measures tend to move together. In the short-run, however, they do not move in lockstep because of sampling differences.

Conference Board. This organization describes itself as a worldwide research and business membership group, with more than 2,700 corporate and other members in 60 countries. The Conference Board survey is ten times larger than the University of Michigan's survey, involving a mail-in survey of 5,000 households. The Conference Board employs NFO Worldwide to conduct this survey, and NFO mails a questionnaire to an entirely different sample of individuals each month. The answers to these questions are used to construct three series: the present situation index, the expectations index, and the consumer confidence index. The consumer confidence index (CCI) is a weighted average of the current and expectations index. Since the CCI is defined as two fifths of the present situation index plus three fifths of the expectations index, it is slightly more weighted to expectations six months ahead. The consumer confidence index is released on the last Tuesday of the month at *www.conference-board.org*.

University of Michigan. The Survey Research Center at the University of Michigan interviews 500 consumers by telephone each month. A broad range of questions is asked about the economy and the purchase of big-ticket items. The responses to these questions are summarized and developed into three indexes: the index of consumer sentiment, the index of consumer expectations, and the index of current economic conditions. The index of consumer expectations is one of the ten series in the Conference Board's Index of Leading Economic Indicators (see Key 15).

The University of Michigan Survey Research Center discloses preliminary interim results (based upon about half the eventual sample of 500 calls) to its clients on a confidential basis in the middle of the month. The results are generally leaked to the financial press and become common knowledge.

Do not be misled by monthly changes in consumer confidence numbers. Focus on the trend in consumer confidence rather than on a one-month change. Both surveys tend to move in similar directions over time but may diverge in any one month. On a monthly average basis, the Michigan survey is more volatile, probably because of the smaller sample size. Another difference is that the Conference Board series seems to increase more rapidly at business cycle peaks when employment prospects improve. Finally, use these numbers skeptically. Wait for actual spending data to confirm these preliminary indications.

25

FOREIGN EXCHANGE

The price at which one currency can be traded for another is the foreign exchange rate. For example, suppose the U.S. exchange rate for the Canadian dollar is $.67. This number means that it takes $.67 of U.S. dollars to buy one Canadian dollar (i.e., 67¢ equals one Canadian dollar). An alternative interpretation is that it takes $1.47 Canadian dollars to buy one U.S. dollar.

The lower the cost of the Canadian dollar in terms of the U.S. dollar, the lower the foreign exchange rate, and vice versa. By the same token, the lower the dollar exchange rate, the cheaper Canadian goods are in the U.S. and the costlier U.S. goods are in Canada.

A foreign exchange rate is a price and, like most prices, is determined by the interaction of supply and demand. Shifts in supply and demand cause foreign exchange rates to change. These shifts can be caused by factors such as changes in tastes, inflation, income, interest rates, and political outlook, in addition to technological improvements, weather, wars, speculation, and so forth.

Fixed Versus Flexible Rates. Exchange rate movements are of special concern to governments because they affect the value of all goods and services traded internationally and, as a result, redistribute income across national boundaries. For many years, a system of fixed exchange rates prevailed internationally. This system meant that governments intervened to prevent foreign exchange rates from changing. Adherents believed that reducing the uncertainty of exchange rates would stimulate international trade and investment. A system of relatively fixed exchange rates managed by the International Monetary Fund prevailed from the end of World

War II until 1971, when the U.S. dollar was devalued. By 1973, fixed exchange rates were abandoned by most countries.

Currently, a system of managed floating exchange rates applies. Governments allow the forces of supply and demand to determine rates—within limits. They are willing to intervene in the market by buying and selling foreign currencies to offset abrupt changes and to curb undesirable speculation.

Foreign Exchange Quotations. Foreign exchange rates are widely reported in the financial press, as in Exhibit 11. The table provides the rates expressed both as dollars per unit of foreign currency and as units of foreign currency per dollar. These rates apply to transactions among banks that involve amounts equal to or greater than $1 million. The rates for smaller transactions are less favorable.

Most international trade involves a delay between setting the price of a transaction and receiving payment. As a result, one of the parties to such a transaction will lose money if the exchange rate changes by the due date. This risk can be reduced by purchasing or selling foreign currency for future delivery at a specified exchange rate (see Key 25). Large transactions of this kind can be handled through banks in what is called the forward market. The 30-, 90-, and 180-day forward rates for various currencies also are reported in Exhibit 11.

EXHIBIT 11
Currency Trading
Monday, January 3, 2000
Exchange Rates

The New York foreign exchange mid-range rates below apply to trading among banks in amounts of $1 million and more, as quoted at 4 P.M. Eastern time by Reuters and other sources. Retail transactions provide fewer units of foreign currency per dollar. Rates for the 11 Euro currency countries are dervived from the latest dollar-euro rate using the exchange ratios set 1/1/99.

Country	U.S. $ equiv.		Currency per U.S. $	
	Mon	Fri	Mon	Fri
Argentina (Peso).............	1.0002	1.0001	.9998	.9999
Australia (Dollar)............	.6582	.6560	1.5192	1.5244
Austria (Schilling)..........	.07462	.07318	13.402	13.665
Bahrain (Dinar)	2.6525	2.6525	.3770	.3770
Belgium (Franc)..............	.0255	.0250	39.2885	40.0615
Brazil (Real).....................	.5495	.5536	1.8200	1.8065
Britain (Pound)................	1.6371	1.6153	.6108	.6191
1-month forward..........	1.6373	1.6156	.6108	.6190
3-months forward........	1.6373	1.6154	.6108	.6190
6-months forward	1.6368	1.6148	.6109	.6193
Canada (Dollar)..............	.6913	.6924	1.4465	1.4442
1-month forward..........	.6919	.6929	1.4453	1.4432
3-months forward........	.6929	.6939	1.4433	1.4411
6-months forward	.6943	.6954	1.4404	1.4381
Chile (Peso) (d).............	.001894	.001888	527.85	529.75
China (Renminbi)............	.1208	.1208	8.2798	8.2795
Colombia (Peso).............	.0005306	.0005333	1884.50	1875.00
Czech. Rep. (Koruna)......				
Commercial rate	.02814	.02793	35.541	35.805
Denmark (Krone)	.1379	.1353	7.2491	7.3933
Ecuador (Sucre)...............				
Floating rate	.00004598	.00004866	21750.00	20550.00
Finland (Markka)	.1727	.1694	5.7908	5.9047
France (Franc)	.1565	.1535	6.3887	6.5143
1-month forward..........	.1569	.1539	6.3736	6.4995
3-months forward........	.1576	.1545	6.3460	6.4710
6-months forward	.1586	.1555	6.3054	6.4297
Germany (Mark).............	.5250	.5149	1.9049	1.9423
1-month forward..........	.5262	.5160	1.9004	1.9379
3-months forward........	.5285	.5183	1.8921	1.9294
6-months forward	.5319	.5216	1.8800	1.9171
Greece (Drachma)	.003113	.003050	321.26	327.83
Hong Kong (Dollar)	.1286	.1286	7.7763	7.7735
Hungary (Forint)	.004034	.003957	247.90	252.71
India (Rupee)...................	.02302	.02299	43.435	43.500
Indonesia (Rupiah)..........	.0001417	.0001431	7055.00	6987.50
Ireland (Punt)	1.3040	1.2789	.7669	.7819
Israel (Shekel)	.2436	.2407	4.1053	4.1548

Country	U.S. $ equiv. Mon	U.S. $ equiv. Fri	Currency per U.S. $ Mon	Currency per U.S. $ Fri
Italy (Lira)	.0005303	.0005201	1885.83	1922.91
Japan (Yen).......................	.009843	.009792	101.60	102.12
1-month forward..........	.009893	.009843	101.08	101.59
3-months forward........	.009989	.009937	100.11	100.64
6-months forward........	.010141	.010088	98.61	99.13
Jordan (Dinar)	1.4085	1.4085	.7100	.7100
Kuwait (Dinar)	3.2895	3.2862	.3040	.3043
Lebanon (Pound)..............	.0006634	.0006634	1507.50	1507.50
Malaysia (Ringgit)	.2632	.2632	3.8000	3.8001
Malta (Lira)	2.4643	2.4254	.4058	.4123
Mexico (Peso)				
Floating rate................	.1063	.1055	9.4050	9.4750
Netherlands (Guilder)......	.4659	.4569	2.1463	2.1885
New Zealand (Dollar)......	.5255	.5229	1.9029	1.9124
Norway (Krone)	.1266	.1248	7.8969	8.0105
Pakistan (Rupee)	.01927	.01930	51.890	51.815
Peru (new Sol).................	.2840	.2850	3.5215	3.5085
Philippines (Peso)............	.02503	.02481	39.950	40.300
Poland (Zloty)	.2418	.2418	4.1350	4.1350
Portugal (Escudo)............	.005121	.005023	195.26	199.10
Russia (Ruble) (a)	.03643	.03630	27.450	27.550
Saudi Arabia (Riyal)........	.2666	.2666	3.7508	3.7510
Singapore (Dollar)...........	.6038	.6004	1.6562	1.6655
Slovak Rep. (Koruna)......	.02427	.02373	41.202	42.132
South Africa (Rand)	.1632	.1625	6.1288	6.1550
South Korea (Won)..........	.0008869	.0008807	1127.50	1135.50
Spain (Peseta).................	.006171	.006052	162.50	165.24
Sweden (Krona)	.1195	.1176	8.3668	8.5030
Switzerland (Franc).........	.6391	.6281	1.5647	1.5921
1-month forward..........	.6416	.6306	1.5585	1.5859
3-months forward........	.6459	.6347	1.5483	1.5755
6-months forward........	.6527	.6414	1.5321	1.5592
Taiwan (Dollar)	.03188	.03186	31.365	31.385
Thailand (Baht)	.02702	.02655	37.015	37.665
Turkey (Lira)	.00000185	.00000184	539255.00	542400.00
United Arab (Dirham)	.2723	.2723	3.6729	3.6730
Uruguay (New Peso)				
Financial	.08608	.08611	11.618	11.613
Venezuela (Bolivar).........	.001540	.001541	649.25	648.75
	— — —			
SDR	1.3761	1.3710	.7267	.7294
Euro	1.0268	1.0068	.9739	.9932

Special Drawing Rights (SDR) are based on exchange rates for the U.S., German, British, French, and Japanese currencies. Source: International Monetary Fund

a-Russian Central Bank rate. Trading band lowered on 8/17/98. b-Government rate. d-Floating rate; trading band suspended on 9/2/99.

The 3-month and 6-month forward rates for France, Germany, Japan, and Switzerland appearing in the Foreign Exchange column were incorrectly calculated for the period beginning with August 13 and ending with October 7. Corrected data are available from Readers' Reference Service (413) 592-3600.

26

NEW ECONOMY

In February 2000, the expansion that began in March 1991 became the longest period of continuous growth in U.S. history. This span of 107 months surpassed the record set during the Vietnam War years of 1961–1969. The United States has enjoyed almost 4% average growth since 1994. In the same period, unemployment has fallen from about 6% to 4%.

In the past, with unemployment at such a low level, inflation would be a serious concern. However, this time, it truly is different. Excluding the volatile food and energy sector, consumer inflation in 1999 was only 1.9%, the smallest increase in 34 years.

The economy produced another surprise aside from rapid growth and anemic inflation. To the astonishment of all the experts, instead of the 30 consecutive years of deficits (1969–1998), the budget has moved from deficits to surpluses. The expectation is that the economy, in the absence of changes in taxation and spending policies, will continue to generate increasing surpluses in the future.

Meanwhile, the stock market zoomed upward. The technology-dominated Nasdaq Composite Index sky-rocketed from under 500 in March 1991 to nearly 5,000 at the beginning of March 2000. The Dow Jones Industrial Average, less influenced by the boom in high technology, still went up an impressive 300% in the same period. In the five consecutive years ending 1999, the total return of the S&P 500 exceeded 20% each year. The previous record was three consecutive years.

New Economy. The last decade has witnessed huge investments in information technology; corporations restructuring to cut costs, improve flexibility, and make better use of technology; increasing deregulation, especially in telecom and labor markets; a vibrant venture capital sector and IPO markets to aid innovative companies; and a supportive monetary and fiscal policy. These factors have resulted in what is called the new economy: faster growth, higher productivity, and lower inflation.

Many experts, once skeptical about the durability of the U.S. economic performance, have become convinced as growth has not only continued but has actually accelerated in recent years. After the end of the 1990–1991 recession, job growth remained subdued. Although companies were investing more, they were reluctant to hire additional employees. It was not until the second half of the 1990s that the economy really took off. The hundreds of billions of dollars invested in high tech began to reap the twin benefits of improved productivity and higher profits. Companies actively hired again, consumers regained their confidence and spent accordingly, and the stock market went on a tear. Stocks accounted for over half of household financial assets in 1999, up from 28% in 1989. By 1999, 80 million Americans, 50% of U.S. households, owned stocks, either directly or indirectly through a pension or mutual fund.

Challenges. The new economy has spawned a new set of challenges posed by prosperity itself. Alan Greenspan, head of the Federal Reserve, has complained that the record-breaking performance of the stock market has weakened the Fed's ability to influence the economy through the traditional lever of interest rates.

The GDP grew at an annual rate of 5.7% in the third quarter of 1999 and 5.8% in the fourth quarter, well above the rate that the Fed feels is sustainable without igniting inflation. Meanwhile, the Nasdaq Composite Index had more than tripled in the 18 months up to March 2000. Consumers, feeling wealthier because of their stock market gains, went on a buying spree.

The rapid growth in the economy caused policy makers to fear that bottlenecks in the supply of labor, raw materials, and other inputs might cause runaway inflation. In response, the Fed raised interest rates six times in the ten-month period ending in May 2000.

Conclusion. None of the Fed's concerns disprove the existence of the new economy that provided so many benefits to the great majority of Americans in the 1990s. However, history teaches us that the introduction of the steam engine, the railroad, and the automobile—all of which transformed the economy of their time—did not repeal the business cycle. Although the economy should continue to grow and prosper, we should expect the expansion to be interrupted by periodic pauses and disruptions.

27

MUTUAL FUNDS

For investors who lack the time or expertise to manage an investment portfolio, an excellent investment alternative is to purchase shares in mutual funds. A mutual fund is a pool of commingled funds contributed by many investors and managed by a professional fund adviser in exchange for a fee. Mutual funds are available to meet a wide range of investment objectives, with more than 7,000 funds currently serving the needs of investors. These varied needs are being met by the issuance of funds that specialize in municipal bonds, money markets, growth stocks, small-company stocks, gold stocks, foreign stocks, and so forth.

Millions of Americans are investing in common stocks indirectly through the purchase of mutual funds. The mutual fund industry now controls more money than life insurance companies or savings and loan institutions. In 1999, total investment was about $6 billion, up nearly 300% in just five years. At the end of 1999, about 50% of American households owned a mutual fund, up from only 6% in 1980.

Advantages. Mutual funds offer several advantages that make them attractive to investors:

1. *Diversification.* A diversified portfolio is difficult to achieve when funds are limited. A mutual fund offers the investor the opportunity to participate in an investment pool that can contain hundreds of different securities.

2. *Professional management.* Many investors lack the time or expertise to supervise their investments. Professionals who have the training and

experience to make judgments about stock selection and timing manage mutual finds.

3. *Liquidity*. Funds can be easily traded. Quotes on the current value of funds are readily available in the financial section of most newspapers and on many web sites.

4. *Constant supervision*. Mutual fund managers handle all the details of managing the portfolio. These details include stock transactions, dividends, cash exchanges, rights, and proxy statements. They arrange for dividend payments and update the performance and tax records for each investor.

Types of Funds. Two basic types of funds exist: closed-end funds and open-end (mutual) funds. A closed-end fund is an investment company with a fixed number of shares that trades on an exchange or over the counter. Supply and demand determine share prices, which can be more or less than a share's intrinsic worth (net asset value).

Open-end funds, by far the most popular type of fund, are funds that issue or redeem shares at the net asset value of the portfolio. Unlike closed-end funds, the number of shares is not fixed but increases as investors purchase more shares. These shares are not traded on any market and are always bought or sold at the net asset value of the portfolio. Typically, large mutual fund organizations manage families of funds that may include, for example, one or more growth stock funds, balanced funds, international funds, money market funds, bond funds, and small-company stock funds. Usually an investor may switch from one fund to another within the same family of funds at no cost or for a small fee.

Open-end funds also can be divided into load and no-load funds based upon whether they charge a sales fee when the fund is initially issued. A load fund is often sold by a stockbroker or financial adviser who charges a fee of up to 8.5% of net asset value, which is deducted from the amount of the investment. Thus, a $10,000 purchase of a 5% load fund means that $500 is deducted as a fee and only $9,500 is actually invested.

No-load funds are typically purchased directly from the fund without stockbroker involvement. There is no initial sales charge. Studies have found no evidence that load funds perform better than no-load funds.

Whether a fund is load or no-load should not be confused with the annual operating expenses incurred by funds that are paid by all mutual fund investors. Information about a fund's annual expenses appears near the front of every mutual fund prospectus, the official sales document that must be sent to new investors. On average, diversified stock funds charge 1.45% annually, but the range is from about 0.2% to 3.0%.

Reading Mutual Fund Quotations. Funds are listed under the name of the sponsor, such as AIM Funds (see Exhibit 12). Symbols after the fund name are described in the explanatory notes at the bottom of the page. The net asset value, or fund's share price (established the preceding trading day), is presented in the second column, and the net change from the previous day is shown in the third column. The fourth column displays the year-to-date percentage change, assuming reinvestment of all distributions, but after subtracting annual expenses. Generally, on the first Monday of each month, the *Wall Street Journal* expands its mutual fund quotations to include details of each fund's performance, sales change, annual expenses, and investment objective.

Selecting Mutual Funds. Before purchasing a mutual fund, an investor should check its performance record. *Barron's* publishes special mutual fund surveys quarterly in mid-February, May, August, and November, including articles and performance statistics. *Forbes'* highly regarded survey is published in August or September and features ten-year performance records of all funds, a selective "honor roll" of outstanding funds, and a ranking of how funds have performed in up and down markets. In February of each year, *Business Week* publishes a scoreboard that assigns ratings to mutual funds that weigh five years of total returns against the amount of risk taken to make those returns. Finally, *Money* publishes regular articles about mutual funds and extensive quarterly statistics on performance. Incidentally, all of these periodicals have excellent web sites.

EXHIBIT 12
Mutual Fund Quotations

Name	NAV	Net Chg	YTD %ret	Name	NAV	Net Chg	YTD %ret
AIM Funds C:				PrGrthB †	34.54	+0.19	+ 28.1
AdvFlex †	17.58	+0.02	− 1.6	QusarB †	25.21	+0.56	+ 12.0
AdvIntV †	19.80	+0.09	+ 21.6	ReEInvB †	9.28	+0.01	− 7.3
AdvLgCp †	21.70	+0.05	− 0.7	SelPremB p	15.78	+0.13	+ 36.1
AdvRlEst †	10.62	+0.05	− 3.5	TechB †	121.57	+0.98	+ 70.6
Bal p	32.65	+0.17	+ 18.1	UtilInc †	16.55	+0.10	+ 17.2
BlChip p	51.12	+0.27	+ 24.8	WldPrivB †	14.40	+0.05	+ 55.1
CapDev †	18.72	+0.30	+ 26.7	**Alliance Cap C:**			
Chart †	18.28	+0.17	+ 32.8	Allian †	6.71	+0.11	+ 32.7
Const†	39.62	+0.56	+ 43.2	BalanC †	14.39	+0.04	+ 4.2
DentTred †	15.40	+0.14	NS	CpBdC †	12.35	−0.01	+ 1.2
GlAgGr †	27.79	+0.26	+ 69.6	GlbDlGvC p	6.60	+0.08	+ 25.6
GlGr †	27.67	+0.14	+ 51.3	GovtC †	6.92	−0.03	− 3.8
Hyld p	8.05	...	+ 1.4	GrIncC †	3.56	+0.01	+ 9.9
Inco †	7.57	−0.02	− 3.7	GwthC †	42.76	+0.43	+ 24.7
IntGov †	8.79	−0.02	− 2.6	HiYldC p	8.95	−0.06	− 2.6
IntlEq †	26.97	+0.11	+ 53.8	InsMuC †	9.18	+0.01	− 7.2
Valu †	47.22	+0.37	+ 28.9	IntlC †	18.79	+0.05	+ 33.7
Weing †	28.87	+0.25	+ 33.8	LtdMtGC †	8.95	−0.22	− 1.8
AIM Global Theme:				MMSC †	6.26	...	+ 1.8
Intl †	16.00	+0.08	+ 51.7	Vista	22.15	+0.56	+119.1
SmCo †	13.60	+0.22	+ 30.6	**American Century Inv:**			
Aetna Class I:				AZIntMu	10.18	...	− 1.0
Ascent	12.13	+0.07	+ 14.8	Balanced	17.22	+0.05	+ 10.1
Balanced	13.86	+0.05	+ 12.3	Bond	8.99	−0.03	− 2.1
Bond	9.82	−0.02	− 0.9	CaHYMu	9.01	...	− 3.3
Crossrds	11.72	+0.04	+ 10.4	CaInsTF	9.59	...	− 4.4
Grwth	23.13	+0.17	+ 35.1	CaIntTF	10.67	...	− 1.1
GrwIncm	14.97	+0.08	+ 17.9	CaLgTF	10.47	...	− 5.2
IndPILgCpl	19.16	+0.08	+ 24.5	CaLtdTF	10.17	...	+ 1.1
Intl	16.04	+0.08	+ 52.1	EmgMkl	6.99	+0.13	+106.2
Legacy	10.40	+0.02	+ 7.5	EqGro	26.23	+0.17	+ 18.5
SmCo	14.00	+0.24	+ 31.0	EqInc	5.60	+0.03	− 0.2
Alger Funds A:				EqIndex	5.87	+0.02	NS
CapApr	15.95	+0.12	+ 74.0	FlintMu	10.13	+0.01	− 0.6
Growth	14.96	+0.07	+ 33.7	Gift	37.92	+0.69	+ 87.3
MidCpGr	25.28	+0.25	+ 35.3	Gl Grwth	9.81	+0.05	+ 86.1
SmCap	10.68	+0.18	+ 32.7	GlGold	5.29	...	− 3.2
Alger Funds B:				GNMA	10.14	−0.03	+ 0.9
Balncd p	20.83	+0.06	+ 25.6	Grwth	32.28	...	+ 34.7

Over the last decade, both the *New York Times* and the *Wall Street Journal* dramatically improved their coverage of mutual funds. These newspapers, along with *Investor's Business Daily*, do an excellent job of providing current data on mutual funds. They also present performance statistics that enable the investor to compare the different funds. The best known source of mutual fund information is *Morningstar*, which provides limited free mutual fund and other financial data and research on its web site at *www.morningstar.com*. The premium service costs $9.95 per month. Those investors wanting an in-depth discussion of mutual funds should read John Bogle's *Common Sense on Mutual Funds* (John Wiley & Sons, 1999).

28

MONEY MARKET FUNDS

A safe place to park your savings is in money market mutual funds. Money market funds are mutual funds that invest in short-term debt instruments. These include government securities, bank certificates of deposit, and commercial paper (short-term corporate IOUs). Commercial paper typically composes half of a taxable money market fund's portfolio. Because money funds are required by the SEC to invest in debt instruments that mature in 90 days or less, there is relatively little risk of default on those loans.

Although money market funds are designed to keep a stable share price of $1, the yield will vary as the general level of interest rates changes. Money market funds often pay substantially more than a regular savings or checking account. In addition, you can usually earn about 1% more than by keeping your savings in a bank money market deposit account.

Although money market funds are relatively safe, they are not entirely risk free. Unlike bank money market deposit accounts, which are federally insured up to $100,000, money funds are not insured. In 1995, two dozen funds used bailouts or insurance to avoid money fund losses after the Orange County bankruptcy. The parent companies absorbed the losses so that the funds' share value would not drop below $1.

Although these investments are not foolproof, no one has lost money in a true money fund. Those investors unwilling to assume any risk can still buy money funds that invest only in government securities, such as Vanguard Money Market Trust Federal Portfolio (800-622-7447). Although you will have to sacrifice some yield in return for their greater safety, their return will still exceed that of most bank money market deposit accounts.

Some money funds pay significantly higher yields than others. Although you might assume that this difference is caused by the higher-yielding funds putting their investors' money into riskier securities, this difference may not be true. The most significant factor causing the difference among funds is the management and operating fees they charge. Expense charges produce almost two thirds of the variation in money fund yields.

The average money fund's expense ratio (annual expenses as a percentage of assets) is about 0.75%. This ratio indicates that a fund earning 5% in interest from its securities would yield a return to its investors of 4.25%. Expense charges can range as high as 1.5% to as low as about 0.30%. In other words, you could easily boost your return by more than half a percentage point by switching into funds with lower expenses.

Some funds have temporarily waived their fees altogether in order to attract new business. This special offer helps new funds to grow rapidly. Large funds are desirable because fixed operating costs can be spread over a broader shareholder base, and the fund manager's personal return increases because the return is typically set as a percentage of assets. You should be aware that once the promotion ends, the manager's fee could sharply increase.

The dividends you earn on most money market funds are fully taxable. Those investors in a high tax bracket might find tax-exempt money funds more attractive. Like all other money funds, they invest in short-term debt securities, and their share prices remain at $1. However, tax-free funds buy only municipal securities, which generally are exempt from federal tax.

Before investing in a tax-free money fund, you should calculate the taxable equivalent yield. This process involves two steps:

Step 1. Subtract your tax bracket from 1. Assuming you are in the 28% tax bracket, the answer is 0.72.

Step 2. Divide the tax-free yield that the fund is paying by the answer you get in Step 1 or 0.72. If the tax-free yield is 3%, divide 3% by 0.72. The answer, 4.17%, is the taxable equivalent yield (yield on a taxable fund).

If you live in a state with high income taxes, you can further reduce taxes by investing in single-state tax-free funds. These funds let you skip state, as well as federal, taxes by investing only in securities issued by municipalities in one state. Most states exempt their residents from state income tax on municipal securities issued in that state. Therefore, the interest from single-state funds is free of state taxes as well as federal taxes for residents of that state. Moreover, if you live in a county or city that has an income tax, the interest is generally exempt from their local taxes.

29

INDEX FUNDS

The hottest strategy in mutual fund investing is buying index funds. An index fund is simply a mutual fund with a portfolio designed to track a broad-based index, such as Standard & Poor's 500 Index or the Wilshire 5000 Index. Over the past three years, investors have poured money into these funds and currently about a quarter of the money invested in mutual funds is targeted to index funds. Vanguard Group's S&P Fund has been the best-selling fund in the United States for the last three years, and with over $100 billion at the beginning of 2000 is currently the largest mutual fund (Fidelity Magellan is the second).

Performance. Why has indexing triumphed as a strategy for investing in mutual funds? The numbers tell the story. The average diversified U.S. stock fund produced a robust 26% return in 1999, easily outdistancing the 21% return of the S&P 500. That year was the first year since 1993 that the average U.S. diversified stock fund beat the index. However, mutual fund performance varied widely. While 20 different stock funds gained 200%, another 10 funds actively fell more that 25%. Viewed differently, the S&P still outperformed about 53% of diversified U.S. stock funds. In 1998, the S&P 500 Index outperformed 86% of all general equity funds. The year before that it was 95%; in 1996, it was 75%. Just 15% of all U.S. diversified funds beat the S&P 500 Index during the period from 1996 to 1999. Typically, a broad capitalization-weighted index can be expected to outperform about two thirds of the actively managed funds. Moreover, the evidence indicates that mutual fund managers who beat the index in one period are unlikely to beat the index in the next period. The past records of funds have not been a good predictor of how they will do in the future.

Cost Advantage. The biggest advantage of indexing and the primary reason for the difference in performance between active and passive investing is the substantially lower cost of index funds. Each dollar incurred in costs cuts the earnings of a fund by a dollar. Index funds are characterized by paltry expense ratios and minimal transaction costs, which translate into higher long-run performance. Vanguard's S&P 500 Fund has an expense ratio of 0.18%, way below the typical equity fund ratio of 1.45%. In addition, active managers replace an average of 90% of the stocks they own each year. This number is referred to as the fund's turnover rate. The turnover rate of an index fund is as low as 5%. Thus, actively managed funds normally incur far greater transaction costs than their indexed competitors. These trading costs for actively managed funds amount to 1.0 to 1.35% of assets versus a typical 0.25% of assets for an index fund. Lower expense ratios and trading costs give index funds a 2.0 to 2.5% cost advantage that is difficult for actively managed funds to overcome.

Tax Advantage. Because S&P 500 and Wilshire 5000 Index Funds have minimal portfolio turnover rates, taxable distributions are much lower. When an actively managed fund trades, capital gains are realized. Active managers often run their funds with little regard for the tax consequences of trading. In good years, large gains often are realized and distributed to stockholders. In contrast, S&P 500 and Wilshire 5000 Funds are highly tax efficient because they rarely sell securities.

Selection. The Vanguard Group (800-635-1511) pioneered index funds and has been by far the largest seller of these funds to the individual investor. The Vanguard Group is known for an emphasis on minimizing costs, and no index fund should be picked that has an expense ratio exceeding 0.40%. Besides Vanguard, Fidelity

Investments (800-544-8888), T. Rowe Price Associates (800-638-5560), and Charles Schwab (800-435-4000) all offer index funds.

With index funds, results are still dependent upon the vagaries of the market. But they provide some level of comfort in that investors know they will not badly lag behind the averages. However, it should be understood that in a down market, they also will decline with the overall market.

The S&P 500 Index has been dominated by large-capitalization (market price per share times the number of common shares outstanding) companies such as Microsoft, Dell, Cisco, and General Electric. Stocks of large-cap companies have performed particularly well over the last decade and have been a major factor in the stellar achievement of the S&P 500 Index. Meanwhile, small-cap stocks have generally been in the doldrums. Investors who expect small-cap stock returns to improve relative to those of large-cap stock should use a total stock market fund as the core index holding.

Total stock market funds track the Wilshire 5000 Index, which, despite its name, includes about 7200 domestic stocks with readily determinable prices. The Wilshire 5000 Index comprises about 99% of the U.S. equity market, while the S&P 500 includes about 80%. Because the Wilshire 5000 Index includes many small-cap stocks, it would reflect an improvement in the returns of the small-cap sector. John Bogle, former chairman of Vanguard Group, recommends this index as the best way to mimic the U.S. stock market. Incidentally, over the last five years the Vanguard Total Stock Market Fund has advanced an annual average of 26.8%, only modestly behind the 28.5% gain of Vanguard's S&P Fund. The difference was caused by the lagging performance of stocks in the small-cap sector.

Although international index products are fewer in number, two good choices are (1) the Vanguard Total International Stock Fund and (2) the Schwab International

Index Fund. The Schwab Fund is more focused on developed countries and has gained an annual average of 15.7% over the last five years. Although this performance may seem unexciting, keep in mind that the international markets have badly underperformed the U.S. markets over the same period.

Indexing can be especially fruitful for those investors buying bonds to help cushion any downturn in the stock market. An intermediate-bond index fund is an especially good choice. Active managers can add little value in picking bonds, so minimizing expenses is even more critical than in selecting stocks. That is why the Vanguard Total Bond Market Fund with an expense ratio of 0.20% is such a good choice. This fund has returned an average of 7.6% annually over the past five years and consistently ranks in the top 20% of its category.

30

MUTUAL FUND PROSPECTUS

The prospectus is the single most important document produced by a mutual fund, and every investor should examine a prospectus before buying a mutual fund. Before a fund will accept your initial order, you must acknowledge that you are familiar with the prospectus. Further, current shareholders must receive new prospectuses when updated (at least once every 14 months).

The prospectus is organized into sections and must cover certain specific topics. The descriptions can seem very technical, but there is good reason for this precision. The prospectus is an official document that requires SEC approval. The SEC has strict guidelines on what can be said in a prospectus and how information must be presented on past performance, expenses, and fees. But, the SEC's approval of a prospectus does not imply approval of any investment.

In the past five years, the SEC has taken several steps to simplify the information presented in a prospectus. Prospectuses are now easier to read and performance is easier to determine, while the length and complexity has been substantially reduced. In fact, with the support of the SEC, some fund companies are currently providing greatly simplified prospectuses that can easily fit on two sides of a sheet of paper.

The cover of the prospectus usually gives a quick rundown of the fund, including its investment objectives, sales or redemption charges, minimum investment, retirement plans available, address, and phone number.

The body of the prospectus provides a more detailed description.

Near the front is a table that describes all the expenses and fees. The table includes three sections. The first section describes maximum sales charges on purchases and reinvested dividends, deferred sales charges, redemption fees, and exchange fees.

Until the mid-1980s, mutual funds were split between the "loads" (which could charge up to 8.5%) and the "no-loads." A load is a sales commission that goes to whoever sells fund shares to an investor and does not go to anyone responsible for managing the fund's assets. If you invest $1,000 and pay a 5% load, only $950 of your money gets invested. If you purchase a no-load fund, the entire $1,000 is invested for you.

In the past decade, mutual fund companies have introduced a variety of fees and charges, such as "contingent deferred sales charges" and "12b-1" fees. Contingent deferred sales charges are often called exit fees or back-end loads. To illustrate, a fund might charge you 5% of its value if sold within the first year. Each year thereafter your exit fee might drop by 1%. After six years, no redemption fee is charged.

The controversial 12b-1 charge, named for the SEC rule, is meant to help defray marketing and distribution costs. Instead of paying this charge once when you buy the fund (front-end load), or when you sell it (back-end load), you pay this fee annually based upon the total net asset value of the mutual fund. Funds with 12b-1 plans can charge up to a maximum of 0.75% of assets per year, or $.75 per $100 of assets.

The second section of the table describes the annual operating expenses, expressed as a percentage of fund net asset value. These expenses include management fees, 12b-1 fees, and other expenses. All funds charge annual management fees, which generally range from .03% to 2.5% of net assets.

Beginning in May 1998, the SEC required mutual

fund companies to show in a table how fees would affect a hypothetical $1,000 investment, assuming a 5% annual rate of return. This section also indicates the total dollar cost to the investor if his or her shares were to be redeemed at the end of one year, three years, five years, and ten years.

There is no evidence that funds with higher charges deliver better performance than those with reduced fees. Although the expense ratio is not the only thing to consider in buying a fund, this ratio should certainly be a factor. Certainly, an expense ratio of more than 2% is excessive (the average for stock funds is about 1.4%).

One of the most important parts of the prospectus is the section containing condensed financial information, which provides statistics on per share income and capital changes. The per share figures are shown for the life of the fund or ten years, whichever is less.

The per share section summarizes fund financial activities for its fiscal year. The financial changes summarized include increases in net asset value due to dividend and interest payments received and capital gains from investment activity. Decreases in net asset value are caused by capital losses from investment activity, investment expenses, and payouts to fund shareholders in the form of distributions.

The last line in the per share section is the net asset value at the end of the year. The net asset value is calculated by dividing the total assets of the fund by the number of mutual shares outstanding.

The financial ratios at the bottom of the table are important indicators of fund strategy and performance. The expense ratio is the ratio shown in the fund expenses section of the prospectus. The ratio of net investment income to average net assets is similar to dividend yield for a stock and reflects the investment objective of the fund. Bond funds would typically have ratios that are more than four times those of stock funds. The portfolio turnover rate is calculated by dividing the lower of purchases or sales by average net assets. This turnover rate tells you how frequently securities are bought and sold by a fund. The higher the turnover, the greater the brokerage costs incurred by the fund. A 100% turnover rate means the securities in the portfolio have been held for an average of one year while a 50% turnover indicates that securities have been held for an average of two years. The average portfolio turnover rate for a mutual fund is about 85%.

Check to see if the portfolio turnover rate is consistent with the objective of the fund. Aggressive growth mutual funds typically will have higher portfolio turnover rates, whereas conservative funds will have lower portfolio turnover rates. In addition, you would like to see a fairly consistent turnover rate over time. A consistent turnover rate is an indication that the portfolio manager is adhering to the investment objective of the fund.

The investment objective section of the prospectus describes the types of investments the fund will make and the amount, in percentage, of assets the fund will normally invest in certain types of investments. This section indicates whether the fund is seeking capital appreciation or income, and often includes the investment philosophy of the portfolio manager, a description of how he or she selects securities, and the anticipated level of portfolio turnover.

The fund management section names the investment adviser and provides a schedule of compensation for the adviser. Most advisers are paid based upon a sliding scale that decreases as assets under management increase. Beginning December 11, 1999, the SEC requires funds to list the names and compensation of their directors in the prospectus. If you want additional information about a fund's officers and directors, including a short biography, you can request what is called a statement of additional information (SAI) from the mutual fund company. The SAI also discloses how much the fund pays in brokerage commissions and other details like shareholder voting rights no longer included in the prospectus.

Following the financial highlights, there is a short section on fund performance that shows the average annual total returns and cumulative total returns for the fund during various periods. The fund performance is also compared to the S&P 500 Index and a peer-group index. Another important table shows the fund's returns year by year and again compares these returns to those of several indexes.

31

DIAMONDS, SPIDERS, AND iSHARES

In recent years, index funds, which are mutual funds that track a market index, have outperformed the great majority of actively managed mutual funds. As a result, money has poured into these funds, making them the hottest sector of the mutual fund industry.

Index funds, however, do not offer the same trading flexibility as traditional common stocks. Mutual funds are bought or sold only at the end of the day when the net asset value is established. If an order is placed for a fund in the morning, what the net asset value will be at the end of the day is conjecture. Meanwhile, common stocks can be traded at any time during the trading day. For this reason, the AMEX created a series of exchange-traded index funds. These products combine many of the advantages of index funds with the superior trading flexibility of common stocks.

Spiders. In January 1993, the AMEX created an index product termed Standard & Poor's Depositary Receipts—SPDRs, called spiders. The spider based on the S&P 500 Index has a symbol "SPY" and holds shares of all the companies in the S&P 500, closely tracking the price performance and dividend yield of the index. The share price of each spider is equal to about a tenth of the S&P 500. So if the S&P 500 were trading at 1,400, each spider would trade at around 140. The annual management fee is a paltry 0.18%, much less than the average stock fund of 1.40%

Spiders also have the advantage of being tax efficient. At the end of the year, mutual funds compute their capital gains from buying and selling stocks, and these gains are then distributed to the individual fundholders. The fundholders are required to pay capital gains taxes on these distributions. However, since index funds rarely trade stocks, they pay little in capital gains.

Spiders have become so popular that they are among the most actively traded listings on the AMEX. These investments enable investors to buy or sell the entire portfolio of the 500 huge companies making up the S&P 500 as easily as trading shares of stock. In addition, spiders also pay quarterly cash dividends representing dividends accumulated on the stocks of the S&P 500 held in trust, less fees and expenses. Finally, for those interested in investing in smaller companies, the AMEX has spiders that track the S&P Mid-Cap 400 Index under the symbol MDY.

iShares. In 1996, the AMEX expanded its index offerings by launching WEBS (World Equity Benchmark Shares), which are designed to give investors fast and economical access to international equity markets. In 2000, these indexes were renamed iShares. Through a single security, investors can own a diversified foreign country stock portfolio that seeks to track the performance of a major benchmark index. Each iShares series represents an investment in a portfolio of publicly traded stocks in a selected country. Investment results are sought that correspond to the price and yield performance of a specific Morgan Stanley Capital International Index (MSCI). MSCI indexes are leading country index benchmarks widely used by U.S. investors for their international investments.

Unlike American depositary receipts (ADRs) that provide an investment in just one company, shares of iShares offer targeted exposure to a portfolio of publicly traded foreign stocks in a selected country. Currently, shares embrace 22 country-specific series of securities (e.g., Germany and Japan).

Diamonds. Diamonds are exchange-traded funds that

track the Dow Jones Industrial Average (DJIA), the most widely publicized of the U.S. stock indexes. The DJIA consists of 30 giant companies with stocks that account for close to a quarter of the stock market's total value. Although professionals use the S&P 500 as their favorite benchmark, over longer periods the DJIA tracks the S&P 500 quite closely. From the beginning of 1980 through the end of 1999, both indexes gained about 14% a year.

Diamonds are popular with individuals who use them as a simple tool for making broad bets on the direction of the market. Institutional investors have directed their attention much more to spiders.

Nasdaq-100 Index. The first product introduced after the combination of the Nasdaq and the AMEX in 1998 was the March 1999 introduction of one based on the Nasdaq-100 Index (QQQ). This product is similar to spiders and diamonds in that it acts like an index fund, but tracks like a stock. These shares have become the most actively traded security on the AMEX because the Nasdaq is dominated by the stocks of companies in the high-technology industry, whose growth has been particularly explosive in the 1990s. The Nasdaq Composite Index advanced about 790% in the 1990s, culminating in a stunning gain of 85.6% in 1999, a record yearly gain for any major market index.

32

MARKET EFFICIENCY

After the stock market crash of October 19, 1987, when the Dow Jones Industrial Average plunged a record 22.6%, articles in *Forbes, Fortune*, and the *Wall Street Journal* discussed the efficient market hypothesis (EMH) and the insight it offered into reasons for the decline. Although the EMH has been a topic of academic interest and debate for the past 35 years, only recently has the hypothesis received the attention of the financial press. Market efficiency is a description of how prices in competitive markets react to new information. An efficient market is one in which prices adjust rapidly to new information and in which current prices fully reflect all available information. The adjustment in stock prices occurs so rapidly that an investor cannot use publicly available information to earn above-average profits. According to the EMH, market prices already reflect public information contained in balance sheets, income statements, dividend declarations, and so forth. Thus, fundamental analysis cannot produce investment recommendations to earn above-average profits. Nor is there much value in technical analysis (see Keys 33 and 34).

Evidence. Although the EMH provides important lessons for investors, its adherents may overstate their case. Several points should be emphasized. First, although much empirical evidence supports the EMH, several strategies have been able to beat the market consistently, and thus are exceptions to the market's efficiency. A market, rather than being perfectly efficient or inefficient, is *more or less* efficient. Generally speaking, efficiency is a function of how closely a market is followed. The case for the efficiency of stock prices on the

New York Stock Exchange (NYSE) is undoubtedly stronger than for those in the over-the-counter market because most of these latter stocks are not monitored as closely. Second, market efficiency varies depending upon the qualifications of investors. For the majority of investors, the market is an efficient mechanism. However, there are investors who do generate above-average returns on a consistent basis. This performance by a minority of investors should not obscure the fact that the performance of mutual funds and the recommendations of investment newsletters indicate that it is difficult to earn above-average profits on a consistent basis. The EMH is therefore an aggregate concept applying to the majority of investors or to the market as a whole.

Lessons of the EMH. Although many analysts are dubious about the EMH, the concept does provide some important lessons that should be absorbed by all investors:

1. Tips are almost always of no value. The market processes new information very quickly.
2. A portfolio should not be churned. A strategy that involves frequent purchases and sales of stocks is likely to be a loser because the commission costs eat up any profits an investor might make.
3. Beating the market is difficult. Only a minority of investors can consistently outperform the market. High returns can usually be achieved only through assuming greater risk. However, greater risk raises the probability of increased losses as well as gains.

33

SECURITIES ANALYSIS: FUNDAMENTAL

Fundamental analysis involves an estimate of a security's value (called intrinsic value) by evaluating the basic facts about the company that issued the security. Once the intrinsic value is determined, the amount is compared to the current market price. If the current market price is less than the intrinsic value, a buy recommendation is issued. Alternatively, if the current market price is greater than the intrinsic value, the recommendation is to sell the security.

Intrinsic Value. Intrinsic value is the price at which a security should sell under normal market conditions. This price is determined by evaluating such factors as net assets (assets minus liabilities), earnings, dividends, prospects of future earnings and dividends (or risk), and management capability. Critical to fundamental analysis is the evaluation of earnings, particularly future earnings. Most fundamental analysts cite the expectation of future earnings as the most important intrinsic variable affecting security prices.

Intrinsic value changes as factors that affect stock prices change (e.g., earnings and dividends). Likewise, stock prices change as the economic prospects of a firm change. However, stock prices fluctuate around the intrinsic value if accurately estimated. External factors, such as pessimism or optimism, may cause temporary gaps between the intrinsic value and the actual price of a security. Fundamental analysts believe that they can exploit these gaps.

Most analysts on Wall Street are fundamental analysts. These analysts make recommendations in published reports that are easily obtainable from brokers. Most of the financial web sites, such as *quote.yahoo.com*, *www.quicken.com*, and *www.moneycentral.com,* provide a summary of the number of buys, sells, or holds for each stock. Since less than 1% of analysts' recommendations are to sell, it is generally understood that when an analyst switches from a buy recommendation to a hold, the message really is "Sell, but I'm afraid to say so because the company in question is a client."

Commonsense Style of Investing. Does each of us have knowledge even the experts on Wall Street don't have? Yes, says Peter Lynch, former portfolio manager of Fidelity Magellan, the largest of all mutual funds. In *One Up on Wall Street* (1989), Lynch advocates a commonsense, down-home style of investing. He thinks investors should concentrate on their own neighborhoods—on what they know better than anybody on Wall Street. Ordinary investors can sniff out trends and spot clues months or even years before Wall Street figures them out by being aware of new products that appeal to their families. For example, he cites how his wife, Carolyn, discovered L'Eggs pantyhose at the supermarket and persuaded Lynch to buy stock in the manufacturer, Hanes, which brought him huge profits.

His advice is to read the local newspaper for information about local firms. Look for want ads for new employees, for construction people to work on a new plant or facility. Ask locally about the company—talking to its employees, calling or visiting the company, mining the local media for information. Don't be afraid to ask questions! After digging around, you should be able to deliver a brief monologue on why you think the stock is a winner. Don't underestimate what knowledge of local companies can do for you. Atlanta is full of Coca-Cola millionaires, Rochester of Kodak & Haloid (Xerox) millionaires, Cincinnati of Procter & Gamble millionaires, Seattle of Microsoft millionaires, and so on.

34

SECURITIES ANALYSIS: TECHNICAL

Technical analysis is the attempt to predict future stock price movements by analyzing the past sequence of stock prices. Technical analysts do not consider such factors as monetary and fiscal policies, political environments, industry trends, or company earnings in attempting to predict future stock prices. Their concern is with the historical movement of prices and the forces of supply and demand that affect prices. Technical analysis is frequently contrasted with fundamental analysis, which attempts to measure the intrinsic value of a security and places considerable reliance upon financial statements and economic trends.

The tools and techniques of technical analysis are endlessly varied. However, there seem to be certain procedures that underlie technical analysis:

1. Market value is entirely determined by the interaction of demand and supply.
2. Both rational and irrational factors govern demand and supply.
3. Stock prices generally tend to move in trends that persist for significant periods of time.
4. Changes in trends are caused by the shift in demand and supply.
5. Chart patterns often tend to recur, and these recurring patterns can be used to forecast future periods.
6. Shifts in demand and supply can be detected in charts of stock prices.

Technical Indicators. As mentioned before, there are

numerous rules and techniques used to predict prices. Technical analysis can frequently be looked upon as an arcane art, and evaluating some of the tools is nearly impossible because the interpretation is so subjective. This section discusses several of the techniques that are widely publicized and can be interpreted objectively.

Advisory Service Sentiment. The poll of more than 100 stock market newsletters published by *Investor's Intelligence* categorizes the forecasts as bullish, bearish, or expecting a market correction. In the aggregate, forecasts of investment advisers tend to follow the market's trend rather than to anticipate a change in it. Therefore, when sentiment for a market move becomes strong in a particular direction, a contrary move in the market is expected. High bullish readings in this poll are usually indications of market tops, while low bullish readings are signs of market bottoms. The results of this survey are published in both *Barron's* and *Investor's Business Daily.*

Advances Versus Declines. This vital technical tool is a measure of the number of securities that have advanced and the number of securities that have declined each day. Major newspapers publish these figures. The ratio of advances to declines provides a better indication of the trend of the overall market than an index like the Dow Jones Industrial Average (DJIA), which is composed of only 30 high-quality stocks. This measure of the breadth of the market is particularly important as peaks and troughs. Technicians believe that the market may be near its peak if the DJIA is increasing while the ratio of advances to declines is decreasing. The market may be nearing a trough when the DJIA is declining and the ratio of advances to declines is increasing.

Investment adviser Martin Zweig likes to track this ratio over a ten-day period. He has found that if advances lead declines by a ratio of two to one over such a span (a rare occurrence) and you invested at this time, you would have made abnormally large profits in the months that followed. Thus, momentum tends to be greatest at the beginning of bull markets.

Moving Average Analysis. According to technicians, this analysis provides a way of detecting trends in stock prices. A moving average can be computed not only for stock averages and indexes but also for individual stocks simply by dropping the earliest number and adding in the most recent number. For example, a 200-day moving average is calculated by adding the most recent day's price to the closing prices of the previous 199 days and dividing by 200. The computation of a moving average tends to eliminate the effect of short-term fluctuations and provides a standard against which to compare short-term fluctuations. For example, technicians consider a downward penetration through a moving average line as a signal to sell, particularly when a moving average price is flattening out. On the other hand, analysts are bullish about a stock when the graph of a moving average price flattens out and the stock's price rises through the moving average.

Locating Data. Data for technical analysis is available in both the *Wall Street Journal* and *Investor's Business Daily*. An additional source of invaluable information for technical analysis is *Barron's*. The best source on the Web for charts of stock movements and other technical data is *www.bigcharts.com*. For some excellent free tutorials on technical analysis, see *www.equityanalytics.com*.

35

ADVISORY SERVICES

There may be as many as 500 investment newsletters, with annual subscription prices ranging from $25 to over $1,000 and with a total of about a million subscribers. Recently, online advisory services have proliferated. In their ads, these services often make extravagant claims about the value of their investment advice. Investors should be skeptical about the claims of omniscience on the part of these newsletters. The performance of many of these newsletters can vary dramatically from one year to the next.

Some market gurus can temporarily influence the price of a stock or even of the market as a whole. Joseph Granville flashed a sell-out signal early in January 1981 and was imputed with causing U.S. stocks to lose $38 billion in market value the following day, with volume rocketing to a then record 93 million shares. Unfortunately, for Granville, he continued to be bearish and fell out of favor when the market turned upward in 1982.

Then 1987 was the year of Bob Prechter and the Elliott wave theory, an esoteric technical theory only its adherents fully grasp. He had predicted a bull market for the late 1980s, and when it occurred, many people thought he was the new financial demigod. However, his prediction of a bear market in the 1990s dimmed his reputation and he faded into obscurity. In 1996, he published *At the Crest of the Tidal Wave: A Forecast for the Great Bear Market*.

Many services use a primarily technical approach to evaluate both the market and individual stocks. Technical analysis attempts to predict futures based upon the pattern of past prices (see Key 34). Other services employ a fundamental approach—analyzing earnings, cash flows, asset values, and other basic financial data (see Key 33). Examples of these services include two of the largest: *Value Line Investment Survey* and *The Outlook*, which is published by Standard & Poor's. Specialized services also are available devoted to options, futures, stock charts, small-company stocks, foreign investments, and insider trading.

Evaluating Newsletters. Keep in mind that from year to year the performance success of all newsletters changes. A proper evaluation requires at least a five-year track record. Before purchasing a newsletter, investors might refer to *The Hulbert Financial Digest,* published in February of each year by Mark Hulbert (703-750-9060), which tracks the performance of more than 160 newsletters. Hulbert also writes a column that appears every other Sunday in the *New York Times*, which discusses the newsletter industry.

An inexpensive way to test a variety of services is to accept the sample offer made by Select Information Exchange (212-247-7123), which offers trial subscriptions to four services in its catalogue for $69.

36

TREASURY SECURITIES

The largest fixed-income market is that for U.S. Treasury obligations. These are backed by the full faith and credit of the U.S. government, and therefore offer the investor maximum safety of principal and a guaranteed yield. Although the yield is typically less than on a corporate bond, Treasury securities are the closest approximation to risk-free investments.

The three most popular Treasury securities for individual investors are Treasury bills, Treasury notes, and Treasury bonds. Treasury bills have maturities up to and including 52 weeks. Treasury notes mature between 2 and 10 years, while Treasury bonds mature in 30 years.

Treasury Bills. T-bills are offered by the Treasury with maturities of 13 weeks, 26 weeks, or 52 weeks. These securities are issued every Monday in minimum denominations of $1,000 and in increments of $1,000 above the minimum. Investors bid for them at a discount by offering, for example, $99 for every $100 of T-bills. At maturity, the investor will receive $100. Yields are expressed on an annual basis, so that in the case of a three-month T-bill purchased for $99, the yield would be the discount of $1 divided by the price of $99 and multiplied by four because there are four three-month periods in a year. For this example, the yield would be 4.08%. The gain of $1 is interest income and subject to federal income tax, but is exempt from state and local taxes.

Treasury Notes. T-notes mature between two and ten years. They are issued in $1,000 and in increments of $1,000 with a fixed interest rate determined by the coupon rate specified in the note. The interest earned is paid semi-annually and is exempt from state and local taxes.

Treasury Bonds. T-bonds make up the smallest segment of the federal debt. These bonds mature and repay their face value within a period of 10 to 30 years from the date of issue. They are issued in denominations of $1,000, with larger amounts purchased in $1,000 increments. A fixed rate of interest is paid semiannually, and the interest earned is exempt from state and local taxes. Some of these issues are callable or redeemable prior to maturity. A callable bond is indicated in the newspaper by a hyphen between the call date and the maturity date. For instance, if 2005–09 is listed under "maturity," that means the bond can be redeemed at any time starting in 2005.

In February 2000, the Treasury Department announced a plan to slash the number of Treasury securities it will sell. The Treasury also is considering phasing out the 30-year Treasury bond, the benchmark for long-term interest rates. Henceforth, the ten-year note may become the benchmark for long-term rates. These actions are a result of the budgetary surpluses currently being generated by the federal government.

Reading the Quotes. Exhibit 13 gives an illustration of how T-bonds, T-notes, and T-bills are reported in the *Wall Street Journal*. The price quotations for T-bonds and T-notes are given per hundred dollars of face value. The first column shows the original interest rate, the second column the month of maturity. The third column indicates the year of maturity. The list is chronological.

"Bid" means the mid-afternoon bid price dealers were willing to pay that day. The ask price indicates the dealer selling price. The next column gives the changes in the bid price from the day before. The last column gives the yield or effective return on the investment. This calculation takes into account the original interest rate, the current ask price, and the amount of time left to maturity.

In the bond market, a price of 100 is called par or face value, and each one-hundredth of par is called a point. The minimum price fluctuation is usually 1/32 of a point, called a tick. To avoid the constant repetition of the number 32, a convention in the bond market prevails that figures after a decimal point or hyphen in a price represent 32nds. As a result, a quotation of 95-8 means 95 and 8/32, or 95-1/4.

In the T-bill section, the date under maturity indicates when the bills are to be retired. Under the bid and ask columns, the decimal takes on its customary meaning: 2.90 means 2 and 9/10. The yield column represents the effective total return, and is used for comparison with other investments.

EXHIBIT 13
Treasury Bonds, Notes & Bills
Monday, January 3, 2000

Representative Over-the-Counter quotations based on transactions of $1 million or more.

Treasury bond, note and bill quotes are as of mid-afternoon. Colons in bid-and-asked quotes represent 32nds; 101:01 means 101 1/32. Net changes in 32nds. n-Treasury note. Treasury bill quotes in hundredths, quoted on terms of a rate of discount. Days to maturity calculated from settlement date. All yields are to maturity and based on the asked quote. Latest 13-week and 26-week bills are boldfaced. For bonds callable prior to maturity, yields are computed to the earliest call date for issues quoted above par and to the maturity date for issues below par. *-When issued.

Source: Telerate/Cantor Fitzgerald

U.S. Treasury strips as of 3 P.M. Eastern time, also based on transactions of $1 million or more. Colons in bid-and-asked quotes represent 32nds; 99:01 means 99 1/32. Net changes in 32nds. Yields calculated on the asked quotation. ci-stripped coupon interest. bp-Treasury bond, stripped principal. np-Treasury note, stripped principal. For bonds callable prior to maturity, yields are computed to the earliest call date for issues quoted above par and to the maturity date for issues below par.

Source: Bear, Stearns & Co. via Street Software Technology Inc.

Rate	Maturity Mo/Yr		Bid	Asked	Chg.	Ask Yld.
6⅜	Jan	00n	99:30	100:00	− 1	6.19
5⅜	Jan	00n	99:30	100:00	− 1	5.25
7¾	Jan	00n	100:04	100:06	− 1	5.02
5⅞	Feb	00n	100:00	100:02	− 1	5.21
8½	Feb	00n	100:09	100:11	− 1	5.30
5½	Feb	00n	99:31	100:01	− 1	5.20
7⅛	Feb	00n	100:07	100:09	− 1	5.16
5½	Mar	00n	99:30	100:00	− 1	5.42
6⅞	Mar	00n	100:08	100:10	− 1	5.45
5½	Apr	00n	99:30	100:00	− 1	5.43
5⅝	Apr	00n	99:29	99:31	− 1	5.67
6¾	Apr	00n	100:08	100:10	− 1	5.69
6⅜	May	00n	100:05	100:07	− 2	5.71
8⅞	May	00n	101:06	101:08	− 1	5.30
5½	May	09n	92:12	92:13	− 22	6.60
9⅛	May	04–09	108:22	108:24	− 16	6.77
6	Aug	09n	95:31	96:00	− 28	6.57
10⅜	Nov	04–09	114:14	114:18	− 18	6.80
11¾	Feb	05–10	120:30	121:04	− 18	6.79
10	May	05–10	113:30	114:02	− 20	6.82
12¾	Nov	05–10	128:04	128:10	− 23	6.81
13⅞	May	06–11	135:25	135:31	− 26	6.81
14	Nov	06–11	138:19	138:25	− 28	6.82
10⅜	Nov	07–12	120:21	120:27	− 26	6.89
12	Aug	08–13	132:23	132:23	− 29	6.90
13¼	˙˙ y	09–14	142:2^	143:03	− 36	6.92
12½	Aug	09–14	138:15	138:21	− 36	6.93
11¾	Nov	09–14	134:00	134:06	− 34	6.91
11¼	Feb	15	139:22	139:28	− 46	6.95

TREASURY BILLS

Maturity			Days to Maturity	Bid	Asked	Chg.	Ask Yld.
Jan	06	'00	2	4.02	3.94	+0.70	4.00
Jan	13	'00	9	5.26	5.18	+0.84	5.26
Jan	20	'00	16	5.20	5.12	+0.65	5.20
Jan	27	'00	23	4.95	4.87	+0.29	4.95
Feb	03	'00	30	5.08	5.04	+0.24	5.13
Feb	10	'00	37	5.12	5.08	+0.15	5.18
Feb	17	'00	44	5.12	5.08	+0.15	5.18
Feb	24	'00	51	5.12	5.08	+0.15	5.19
Mar	02	'00	58	5.23	5.19	+0.13	5.31
Mar	09	'00	65	5.24	5.22	+0.12	5.34
Mar	16	'00	72	5.25	5.23	+0.11	5.36
Mar	23	'00	79	5.25	5.23	+0.10	5.36
Mar	30	'00	86	5.27	5.26	+0.08	5.40
Apr	06	'00	93	5.36	5.34	+0.16	5.49
Apr	06	'00	93	5.30	5.29	+0.06	5.44
Apr	13	'00	100	5.33	5.31	+0.14	5.46
Apr	20	'00	107	5.35	5.33	+0.11	5.49
Apr	27	'00	114	5.36	5.34	+0.10	5.51
May	04	'00	121	5.42	5.40	+0.07	5.58
May	11	'00	128	5.43	5.41	+0.05	5.59
May	18	'00	135	5.46	5.44	+0.05	5.63
May	25	'00	142	5.50	5.48	+0.05	5.68
Jun	01	'00	149	5.49	5.47	+0.06	5.67

117

Treasury securities can be purchased directly without paying any commissions by setting up a "Treasury Direct Account" at the Bureau of the Public Debt web site, *www.publicdebt.treas.gov*. The alternative is to purchase the securities through a bank or brokerage firm, where you will be charged a small commission. A nice feature of Treasury Direct is that maturing Treasury bills automatically can be reinvested.

Significance of Interest Rates. The huge volume of T-bills makes them the most important short-term investment. Their yield has become the bellwether of short-term interest rates, just as the yield on T-bonds has been the bellwether for long-term interest rates. The size of this market, the creditworthiness of the federal government, and the popularity of these securities with institutional and foreign investors make Treasury interest rates extremely responsive to changes in economic conditions. In addition, the Fed buys and sells these securities to control the money supply and influence interest rates (see Key 17). As a result, changes in the interest rates paid by the U.S. Treasury affect the interest rates paid by borrowers in North America and around the world.

37

CORPORATE BONDS

Corporate bonds are debt obligations that are secured by specific assets or a promise to pay. In effect, a bond investor lends money to the bond issuer. In return, the issuer promises to pay interest and to repay at maturity.

Many new corporate bond issues with a variety of maturities are ordinarily sold each week. Some of these issues have maturities of approximately a year, while others have maturity lengths of 30 years or more. In 1993, Disney startled the financial world by selling bonds that mature in 100 years.

Because bondholders are creditors, they have a prior claim on the earnings and assets of the issuing corporation, ranking ahead of preferred and common stockholders. Interest must first be paid to the bondholders before dividends can be distributed to stockholders. In case of dissolution or bankruptcy, bondholders have a prior claim on assets over stockholders. Only corporations in extreme financial difficulty will fail to pay the interest on their bonds.

Corporate bonds are typically issued in denominations of $1,000, called the face, par, or maturity value. If an investor buys five bonds, the total face value is $5,000, which means the corporation promises to repay $5,000 when the bonds mature. In addition, the corporation promises to pay interest, generally semiannually at a specified annual rate on the face value. The interest rate is commonly called the coupon or stated rate.

Bonds fluctuate in price, with market value largely determined by changes in interest rates. As the general level of interest rates rises, bond prices go down. Alternatively, as the interest rates decline, bond prices increase. Other factors, such as the bond's rating, also influence price.

Understanding the different definitions of yield is critical to understanding bond pricing. *Coupon yield* is the interest rate stated on the bond. *Current yield* is obtained by dividing the stated interest rate by the latest price. The *yield to maturity* is the most important concept of yield because it is the yield upon which all bond prices are based. The formula takes into account purchase price, redemption value, time to maturity, coupon yield, and the time between interest payments.

Bond Ratings. One of the factors in determining the interest rate a bond must pay to attract investors is the credit quality of the bond. The two most important companies evaluating bonds, Moody's Investors Service and Standard & Poor's, generally reach the same conclusions about each bond. Exhibit 14 provides the risk classifications and a general description of their meaning. Bonds rated AAA by Standard & Poor's or Aaa by Moody's are the highest-grade obligations, meaning they possess the ultimate degree of protection as to principal and interest. Bonds rated below BBB or Baa are speculative in nature and are called junk bonds. These lower-quality bonds must pay higher yields in order to attract investors.

Reading the Quotes. A typical listing from the *Wall Street Journal* will look as follows:

Bonds	CurYld	Vol	Close	NetChg
IBM 8 3/8 19	7.7	15	108 3/8	−1 5/8

The first column shows the name of the issuer and notes of the original interest rate (coupon rate) and the year of maturity. Thus, 8 3/8 19 is interpreted as 8 3/8% bonds due in 2019. The second column gives the current yield, or the interest obtained by dividing the original interest rate by the latest price. In this case, each bond pays $83.75 annual interest, so the current yield is 7.7%. The third column indicates the volume of trading, in thousands of dollars. In this case, $15,000 was traded.

The last two columns provide the closing price and the change from the previous day, which is a decrease of $1.625 per bond.

Bond prices are quoted as a percentage of face value. In our example, the closing price of 108 7/8 means that the actual price of the bond is 108 7/8 × $1,000 face value = $1,088.75 for each bond. In discussion of bonds, the term basis point is often used. A basis point is one-one hundredth of 1 percent and is a convenient way to discuss changes in yields. For example, an increase in yield from 7.5% to 8% is a 50-basis point increase.

EXHIBIT 14
Bond Ratings

Description	Moody's	Standard & Poor's
High Grade	Aaa	AAA
	Aa	AA
Medium Grade	A	A
	Baa	BBB
Speculative	Ba	BB
	B	B
Default	Caa	CCC
	Ca	CC
	C	C

Interestingly, there are far more outstanding bond issues than stock issues and most are in the over-the-counter markets rather than on the exchanges, which makes them more difficult to track. The Bond Market Association estimates that there are 300,000 to 400,000 corporate bonds listed, and most bonds don't trade on a given day.

Online fixed-income activity will probably increase when stocks return to more normal rates of return rather than the 18% annual return of the 1990s. Those wishing to learn more about bonds should check the Bond Market Association web site at *www.investinginbonds.com*. This site includes an excellent educational section, which includes thorough explanations of the different types of bonds, as well as a seven-step online program. Also available are price quotes on U.S. Treasury securities and actively traded municipal and investment-grade corporate bonds.

38

MUNICIPAL BONDS

Municipal bonds are debt securities issued by state and local governments and local government agencies and authorities. Municipal bonds differ from corporate bonds in three significant respects:

1. The interest on municipal bonds is exempt from federal income taxes. In addition, if these bonds are issued in the investor's state of residency, they also are exempt from state and local income taxes. This tax-exempt feature is what makes municipal bonds or "munis" attractive to investors in higher income tax brackets.

2. Most municipal bond issues are serial bond issues as opposed to the term maturities of corporate and Treasury bonds. The advantage of having a portion of the bonds mature periodically over the life of the issue for the issuer is that it spreads fixed principal repayment obligations over a number of years to correspond to the flow of tax revenue receipts.

3. Most municipal bonds are issued in $5,000 denominations, while corporate bonds are issued in $1,000 denominations.

Types of Municipal Bond Issues. Two general types of munis exist: general obligation bonds and revenue bonds. General obligation bonds (GOs) are backed by the full taxing power of the issuer; thus, they are considered the safest munis. Revenue bonds are payable from the revenues generated by a particular project such as a sewer, gas, or electric system, airport, or toll bridge financed by the issue. Because only these revenues are pledged to pay interest and repay the principal, revenue bonds are generally considered to possess higher default risk than GOs. As a result, they usually carry higher yields.

Selecting Municipal Bonds. Standard & Poor's Corporation and Moody's Investors Service are the two major municipal rating agencies. In general, the higher the safety rating the lower the interest, although other factors in addition to rating also affect a bond's price. The symbols used by Moody's and Standard & Poor's are the same symbols used in rating corporate bonds (see Key 37).

For those investors with limited time and resources, the best way to invest in munis is to purchase municipal bond mutual funds. This approach affords the investor diversification as well as constant supervision by professional management. The minimum required investment is usually $1,000.

Price Quotations. The market for municipal bonds is not as liquid as the market for federal government securities. Trading is not active because many of these securities are not listed in large amounts. As a result, the spread between bid and ask prices in this market tends to be larger than for similar federal government issues. Prices on municipal bonds are seldom reported in local newspapers. The *Wall Street Journal* and some other dailies print a short list of the newer, more actively traded issues. The list reveals the name, coupon rate, maturity date of each issue, a representative price, change from the previous day, and the yield to maturity. An investor interested in obtaining specific quotes can refer to a publication such as the *Blue List*. Dealers will give quotes, but they may vary depending on factors such as the dealer's profit margin.

Dramatic revolution, fueled by the Internet, is about to sweep the municipal market. Few municipal bonds are traded in cyberspace so far, but this absence is about to change. MuniAuction, the first municipal auction web site (*www.muniauction.com*), will conduct electronic auctions of new municipal bond issues in real time. Currently, only 25% of new issues are competitively bid. MuniAuction will have underwriters competing for a municipal bond issuance. Competitive bidding should mean more bids and competition with lower interest rates and costs.

Trading Edge's BondLink (*www.tradingedge.com*) is the first online trading service for high-yield bonds. This service lets an investor trade high-yield bonds right from a desktop.

39

FINANCIAL FUTURES

Financial futures are futures contracts written on securities, money, or various stock indexes. A futures contract is an agreement between seller and buyer to respectively deliver and take delivery of a commodity at a specified future date. Investors can use positions in the futures market to protect the gains they have made in the cash market. Speculators can also use futures to profit from anticipated changes in financial markets. Futures are recommended only for sophisticated investors. The majority of individual investors lose money. Some are ruined.

Financial futures are traded on a regulated exchange complete with established rules for the performance of contracts. The exchange clearinghouse acts as a third party and guarantor to all transactions, thus eliminating the need for sellers and buyers to become known to one another. While a future is a commitment to buy or sell at some point in the future, delivery of the underlying instrument rarely occurs. Trades in futures contracts are settled by entering into the offsetting position.

Reading Futures Quotes. Exhibit 15 provides an example of a futures listing. The following terms are used in the exhibit:

Open. Price at which the first bids and offers were made or first transactions were completed.

High. Top offer or top price at which a contract was traded during the trading period.

Low. Lowest bid or lowest price at which a contract was traded.

Settlement. Price brokers use for valuing portfolios.

Net change. Amount of increase or decrease from the previous trading period's settlement price.

Life-of-contract highs and lows. Highest price or offer and lowest price or bid reached in the lifetime of a futures contract for a specific delivery month.

Volume. Number of contracts traded (one side of each trade only) for each delivery month during the trading period.

Open interest. Accumulated total of all currently outstanding contracts (one side only) in futures, referring to unliquidated purchases and sales.

Arithmetic of Financial Futures Trading. Perhaps more than any other form of speculation or investment, gains and losses in futures trading are highly leveraged. The leverage of futures trading results from the fact that only a small amount of money (called margin) is required to buy or sell a futures contract. The smaller the margin in comparison to the value of the futures contract, the greater the leverage. The term *margin* as used in connection with securities refers to the cash down payment a customer deposits with a broker when borrowing from the broker to buy securities. However, when applied to futures, margin is a deposit of good-faith money that can be used by the brokerage firm to cover trading losses. Margin is analogous to money held in an escrow account.

EXHIBIT 15
Financial Futures Price Quotations
INDEX

DJ INDUSTRIAL AVERAGE (CBOT)-$10 times average

	Open	High	Low	Settle	Change	Lifetime High	Lifetime Low	Open Interest
Mar	11635	11715	11415	11453	– 172	11715	10091	10,472
June	11830	11850	11560	11591	– 172	11850	10275	593
Sept	11847	11847	11725	11738	– 172	11847	11282	252
Dec	...	...	...	11897	– 172	12074	8100	206

    Est vol 15,000; vol Fri 2,689; open int 11,523, –11.

    Idx prl: Hi 11522.01; Lo 11305.69; Close 11357.51, –139.61.

S&P 500 INDEX (CME)-$250 times average

	Open	High	Low	Settle	Change	Lifetime High	Lifetime Low	Open Interest
Mar	148850	149650	145200	146680	–1740	149650	97000	356,864
June	151450	151450	147200	148570	–1740	151450	98000	8,474
Sept	153200	153200	149240	150540	–1730	153200	99000	2,309
Dec	...	...	...	152650	–1740	155290	126650	2,155
Mr01	...	...	...	154950	–1740	157590	132430	15
June	...	...	...	157250	–1740	159890	134280	119

    Est vol 100,671; vol Fri 20,963; open int 369,941, +110.

    Idx prl: Hi 1478.00; Lo 1438.36; Close 1455.17, –14.08

The exchange on which the contract is traded sets minimum margin requirements, typically about 5% to 10% of the current value of the futures contract. If the funds in an investor's margin account are reduced below what is known as *maintenance level*, the broker will require that additional funds be deposited. Also, the investor may be asked for additional margin if the exchange or brokerage firm raises its margin requirements. Requests for additional margin are known as margin calls.

Further information on futures can be obtained at the web sites of the two major futures exchanges: the Chicago Board of Trade (*www.cbot.com*) and the Chicago Mercantile Exchange (*www.cme.com*).

40

COMMODITY FUTURES

A commodity futures contract is a contract covering the purchase and sale of physical commodities for future delivery on a commodity exchange. The futures contract requires the future seller to deliver to a designated location a specified quantity of a commodity to be sold to the future buyer at a stipulated price on some defined later date. Originally, the purpose of futures was to transfer risk from one party to another and to smooth out price fluctuations. Subsequently, speculation has become an important factor in these markets. Commodity futures are used primarily by four groups of people:

1. Producers, including farmers, use the futures market to lock in the prices they receive for their products.
2. Commercial consumers use futures to insulate themselves from wide swings in the prices of the commodities they use.
3. Investors use futures as an opportunity to speculate on future price changes, up or down. These speculators theoretically assume the price risk that the hedger is seeking to minimize.
4. Finally, exchange floor traders are middlemen, buying from producers and selling to users.

The Futures Marketplace. The commodity futures market is close to being a purely competitive market, with prices being determined by demand and supply. Usually a variety of forces exist at any one time to move prices up or down. These forces can involve a range of political, social, and economic factors in addition to factors peculiar to the particular commodity. Gold is an example of a commodity whose price is strongly influenced by political factors. However, for most agricultural commodities, fluctuating supplies largely determine prices.

Futures markets function as a form of forward pricing rather than substituting for the actual purchase or sale of a commodity. In fact, only about 2% of all futures contracts result in delivery.

Reading Futures Prices. Exhibit 16 is an example of how futures prices are reported. The top boldfaced line gives the name of the commodity, here, corn. Also listed is the exchange (CBT), which stands for the Chicago Board of Trade. Finally, the line lists the size of a single contract (5,000 bushels) and the way in which prices are quoted (cents per bushel).

The first column gives the months in which the delivery of the contract may occur. The next three columns give the opening, highest, and lowest prices of the day. A blank indicates that a particular month has not traded that day. The fifth column gives the settlement price, the price brokers use for valuing portfolios and for deciding whether to call for more margin. The sixth column shows the difference between the latest settlement price and that for the previous day. The second and third columns from the right display the highest and lowest prices at which each contract has ever traded. The right-hand column reveals the open interest in the contract. Open interest is a measure of the public interest in a contract. Generally, the higher the open interest, the more liquid is the contract—that is, the easier to trade. The bottom line gives the volume of contracts traded, the previous day's volume, the total open interest, and the change from the previous day.

EXHIBIT 16
Commodities Futures Prices

Monday, January 3, 2000
Open Interest Reflects Previous Trading Day

GRAINS AND OILSEEDS

	Open	High	Low	Settle	Change	Lifetime High	Lifetime Low	Open Interest
CORN (CBT) 5,000 bu.; cents per bu								
Mar	204½	205¾	200½	200¾	− 3¾	270	195¼	211,737
May	211¼	212¼	207¾	208	− 3¼	261	202½	61,464
July	217¾	219	214½	214¾	− 3¼	278½	209	58,065
Sept	225	225¼	221¾	222	− 2	257	215¾	16,869
Nov	229	229	228½	228¾	− 2	245	222½	559
Dec	233½	234½	231	231½	− 2¼	279½	225¼	33,477
Mr01	242¾	242¾	239¾	239¾	− 1¾	246½	233¾	869
Dec	253	253½	251½	252	− 1½	263	246½	1,114

Est vol 72,000; vol Fri 0; open int 384,452, +306.

131

41

GOLD

Gold prices hit a 20-year low on September 23, 1999, at $255 an ounce. Within days, gold prices gathered momentum and peaked at $340. What caused this dramatic change? The rise in price and improvement in sentiment were triggered by a joint statement on official gold holdings by the European Central Bank (ECB) and 14 European central banks on September 24, 1999. According to this statement, gold will remain an important element of global monetary reserves, and the central banks have undertaken to restrict their annual sales to 400 tons under a harmonized five-year program.

This declaration of intent should continue to have a positive effect on gold prices because central banks are by far the largest holders of gold. About 30,000 tons of gold are stored in central bank vaults, the equivalent of almost 13 years' output. The potential sale of a large part of the banks' holdings was a serious impediment to any advance in gold prices.

From 1934 to 1971, the United States maintained a policy of buying and selling gold at a fixed price of $35 per ounce. This standard prevailed until the Nixon administration suspended the dollar's convertibility into gold in 1971. Since then, the value of gold has been determined by market forces.

In the 1970s, the price of gold zoomed upward and peaked in 1980 at $612 an ounce before slipping to $308 in 1984. In 1990, its price was $383 and it finished the decade at less than $300. The causes of this anemic performance were low inflation, gold's declining role as a monetary standard, and central bank sales. These factors have all combined to keep a lid on gold prices.

Although estimates can be made of changes in supply, predicting demand is much more difficult. In 1998, more than 80% of the gold produced was used for decorative purposes, 7% for industrial use, and 12% for private investment holdings. Gold has traditionally been a barometer for confidence in political and currency stability. When inflation heats up, demand for gold increases. Purchases of gold also surge when political events take a serious turn, although this response has been muted in recent years. Finally, high interest rates on money market instruments and securities make them more attractive as investments than gold because its ownership yields no interest. All of these factors make forecasting gold prices very difficult.

How to Purchase Gold. If an investor wants to buy gold to ensure against economic instability or to diversify holdings, there are six major avenues that can be pursued: mutual funds, gold stocks, coins, bullion, futures contracts, and options.

Many gold stocks are available on the exchanges as well as over the counter. Because of the uncertainty about gold's future price, one should invest in only the more efficient producers. There also are mutual funds that invest in the stocks of gold-mining companies.

Gold coins are issued by several governments, which guarantee their gold content. These coins come in various weights and sizes. Some have a pure gold content while others consist of gold mixed with copper. Gold coins are sold at prices that reflect their gold value plus a premium of from 5% to 8%. The most prominent gold coins are the American Gold Eagle, South African Krugerrand, Canadian Maple Leaf, Austrian 100 Corona, and the Gold Mexican 50 Peso.

Gold bullion comes in many sizes, ranging from a tiny wafer to 400-ounce bars. Most investors do not actually take physical possession of the bullion. Instead, they purchase a certificate of ownership that indicates the gold is on deposit in a bank. Certificates can be purchased from certain banks, large brokerage houses, and recognized dealers.

Gold futures contracts are speculations that provide tremendous leverage. Typically, the cash requirements are 4% to 10% per contract. If the price falls, the investor is susceptible to a margin call for more cash or collateral. This strategy should be used only by experienced traders familiar with the risks involved.

Gold options do not face the possibility of margin calls. Maximum risk is defined by the premium paid for the option. Like futures, the leverage is high and the profit potential large. However, as with futures, most speculators in options lose money.

Is Gold a Smart Investment? Gold has been a poor investment over the past 20 years. Although the demand for gold (particularly for jewelry) continues to rise and annually exceeds the output produced, this gap is easily filled by the sales of gold from central bank and private holdings. Remember that virtually all of the gold ever mined remains above ground and theoretically could be melted down and used again. A moderation in central bank sales combined with increasing inflation or political instability could improve gold prices in the future. However, most experts recommend investing only 5% to 10% of personal savings in gold investments because of their volatility and high risk.

42

CORPORATE DIVIDENDS

Dividends are distributions to stockholders. Although most commonly in the form of cash or stock, dividends may consist of property. Typically, corporations can only declare dividends out of earnings, although some state laws and corporate agreements permit the declaration of dividends from sources other than earnings. Dividends based on sources other than earnings are sometimes described as liquidating dividends, because they are a return of the stockholders' investment rather than of profits.

Cash dividends are usually paid on a quarterly basis shortly after the dividend resolution has been approved by the board of directors. Dividends cannot be paid immediately because the ongoing purchases and sales of the corporation's stock require that a current list of stockholders be prepared. For example, a resolution approved at the April 10 (declaration date) meeting of the board of directors might be declared payable on May 5 (payment date) to all stockholders of record as of April 25 (record date). In this instance, on April 26, the day after the record date, the stock would trade ex-dividend, usually falling in price to compensate for the fact that the shares no longer qualify for the latest dividend. News of corporate dividends is reported daily in the *Wall Street Journal* and the financial pages of larger newspapers.

Corporations have widely varying dividend policies. Smaller, high-growth companies tend to have lower payout ratios (percentage of earnings paid as cash dividends) than mature companies. Generally, new companies have a stronger need to reinvest the cash generated from operations to finance growth.

Dividend Yield. The dividend yield percentage is

often reported in the stock tables of major newspapers. This number is obtained by dividing the annual cash dividend by the closing price of the stock. The annual cash dividend is based upon the rate of the last quarterly payout. If the dividend in the last quarter was $.25 per share, the annual dividend is assumed to be $1.00.

Stock Splits and Stock Dividends. A stock split is the issuance to stockholders of new shares of stock. A 2 for 1 split, for example, gives each stockholder two new shares for each of the old shares. A stock dividend is simply a small stock split (25% or less). For example, if a corporation issues a 5% stock dividend, the owner of 100 shares will receive an additional five shares of stock. Stock dividends, like cash dividends, trade ex-dividend after the record date. Stock that is split trades both on the pre-split basis and on a when-issued basis (wi) between the declaration date and the record date. Thus, a $100 stock split that was 2 for 1 should carry a $50 wi price.

Stock dividends, rather than cash dividends, are usually issued by smaller companies that need cash for reinvestment purposes. The usual argument for splits is that investors prefer stocks that trade within a range of about $20 to $50. Stocks priced higher require a larger investment to purchase a round lot (100 shares) and therefore limit the number of interested investors.

Although logic would indicate that splits are not meaningful, investors perceive stock splits to have value and tend to react positively to announcements. Most stock splits come after periods of strong price performance, so the company is expressing its confidence in the future through its split announcement. Information about stock splits can be found at *www.briefing.com*, *www.smartmoney.com*, *www.theonlineinvestor.com*, and *quote.yahoo.com*.

Recent History. At the beginning of 2000, the dividend yield on the S&P 500 was 1.2%, an all-time low. It should be remembered that dividends in the past have been a much more significant part of total return. From

1926 through the end of 1999, about 40% of the 11.3% average yearly return on common stocks was attributable to dividends.

The dividend yield is so low for several reasons. First, the bull market of the 1990s has pushed stocks to record levels. The year 1999 marked the fifth consecutive year of double-digit returns, an all-time record. In addition, stockholders often prefer capital gains to dividends because of U.S. tax regulations. Increases in stock prices are not taxed until a stock is sold, and then they are subject to favorable capital-gains rates as low as 10% and no higher than 20%, as long as the stock is held for more than 12 months. Short-term gains from sales of stock are taxed at ordinary income tax rates. Dividends are taxed at ordinary income tax rates as high as 39.6%.

43

CORPORATE ACCOUNTING AND REPORTING

Accounting is the language of business and financial statements and represents a primary medium that corporations use to communicate their progress and performance. Financial statements are issued in a summarized form on a quarterly basis, and complete financial statements with notes are issued annually. Most analysts regard financial statements as a vital source of information about a firm. This Key presents a discussion of two of the three basic financial statements, the *income statement* and the *statement of cash flows*. The *balance sheet* is discussed in Key 45.

Income Statement. The income statement reports the income (also called earnings or profit) for a period of time. Income is the result of subtracting expenses from revenues. Income is divided by the number of common shares outstanding to get earnings per share (EPS), which is disclosed at the bottom of the income statement. Why is the income statement so important? The primary reason is that this statement provides investors, creditors, and others with information to help predict the amount, timing, and uncertainty of future earnings and cash flows. Accurate prediction of future earnings and cash flows permits the assessment of the economic value of the firm, the probability of loan repayment, and the probability of dividend payout.

Financial Ratios. Although there are many financial ratios used by analysts, some of the most prominent ones are based on amounts reported in the income statement. The most widely publicized of all financial ratios, earnings per share, is discussed in Key 44. Other prominent ratios using income statement numbers are as follows:

- *Gross profit margin:* This ratio is computed by dividing gross profit by net sales for the period. The equation for this relationship is

$$\text{Profit margin on sales} \ = \ \frac{\text{Gross profit}}{\text{Net sales}}$$

  This ratio measures the ability of the company to control inventory costs and to absorb price increases through sales to customers.
- *Return on common stock:* This ratio is the ultimate measure of operating success to owners by dividing net income by the equity of common stockholders. In equation form:

$$\begin{array}{c}\text{Rate of return on} \\ \text{common stock} \\ \text{equity}\end{array} \ = \ \frac{\text{Net income} - \text{preferred dividends}}{\text{Common stockholders' equity}}$$

  (To obtain common stockholders' equity, one must subtract from *total* stockholders' equity the stockholders' equity that pertains to preferred stock.)
- *Price-earnings ratio:* The P/E ratio is widely used by analysts in assessing the investment possibilities of different stocks. It is computed by dividing the market price of the stock by the earnings per share:

$$\text{P/E ratio} \ = \ \frac{\text{Market price of stock}}{\text{Earnings per share}}$$

High P/E stocks are usually characterized by greater growth potential than low P/E stocks.

- *Payout ratio:* The payout ratio is the ratio of cash dividends to net income.

$$\text{Payout ratio} = \frac{\text{Dividends per share}}{\text{Earnings per share}}$$

Many investors select securities with a fairly substantial payout ratio. However, other investors are more concerned with growth in sales and profits, leading to appreciation in the price of the stock. High-growth companies tend to be characterized by low payout ratios because they reinvest most of their earnings.

Statement of Cash Flows. The adoption of this statement in 1988 was spurred by the dissatisfaction of many investors with reported earnings as a measure of a firm's performance. Reported earnings are affected by choices made in the accounting methods used and may not be indicative of the underlying cash flows. Earnings also are affected by revenues and expenses that do involve the inflow or outflow of cash.

The primary purpose of this statement is to report information about a company's cash receipts and cash payments. This useful statement provides information about (1) sources of cash during the period, (2) uses of cash during the period, and (3) change in cash balance during the period.

The statement of cash flows is classified into three major categories:

1. Operating activities, which include the typical daily transactions involving the sale of merchandise and the providing of services to customers. Examples include the cash receipts from the sale of goods or services and cash payments to suppliers for purchases of inventory.
2. Investing activities, which include lending money, collecting on those loans, or acquiring and dispos-

ing of productive long-lived assets.

3. Financial activities, which include obtaining cash from creditors, repaying the amounts borrowed, or obtaining capital from owners and providing them with dividends.

Focal Number. The cash flow from operating activities is the first and foremost source of a company's cash from the sale of goods and services. If operating cash flow is not the primary source of a company's cash flow, the company could be in trouble. The bigger the contribution of operating cash flow to a company's cash needs, the better.

44

CORPORATE EARNINGS

Earnings per share (EPS) is the most publicized and relied-upon financial statistic. The financial dailies report earnings for most listed and OTC issues as they are announced. Corporations are required by the SEC to report EPS to their stockholders every three months. Reported earnings can have at least a short-term impact on the price of a stock, particularly when they differ from expectations.

EPS has been called a summary indicator because as a single item it communicates substantial information about a company's performance or financial position. However, misleading inferences can be drawn if the calculations that derive EPS on the income statement are ignored. Further, analysis of a company's total operations and financial condition requires more information than can be garnered by simply examining EPS.

The term *earnings* is synonymous with net income and net profit to accountants who compute EPS. Earnings per share is the net earnings remaining for common stockholders after dividends due to the preferred stockholders:

$$\text{Basic EPS} = \frac{\text{Net income} - \text{preferred dividends}}{\text{Average common shares outstanding}}$$

Complex Capital Structure. The calculation of EPS becomes more complicated when companies have convertible securities, stock options, warrants, or other financial instruments that can be exchanged for or converted to common shares at some future time. The presence of these securities means that there is a potential

142

increase in the number of common shares outstanding. In the computation of EPS, an increase in the number of shares outstanding results in a reduction (or dilution) of EPS. (See Exhibit 17 for sample earnings reports from the *Wall Street Journal*.) A doubling of shares, for instance, results in a 50% reduction of EPS.

EXHIBIT 17 Digest of Earnings Report

Brown & Brown (N)   BRO

Quar Dec 31:	1999	r1998
Revenues..............	$43,343,000	$40,663,000
Net income..........	7,084,000	6,130,000
Avg dil shr	13,712,000	13,771,000
Shr earns (diluted):		
Net income	.52	.45
Year:		
Revenues..............	176,413,000	158,947,000
Net income..........	27,172,000	23,349,000
Avg dil shr	13,736,000	13,704,000
Shr earns (diluted):		
Net income	1.98	1.70

CCF Holding Co. (Sc)   CCFH

Quar Dec 31:	1999	1998
Net income..........	$283,900	$402,630
Shr earns (diluted):		
Net income	.29	a.41
Year:		
Net income..........	1,002,891	618,776
Shr earns (diluted):		
Net income	1.02	a.63

a-Adjusted for a 10% stock dividend paid in 4/99.

CNBT Bancshares (Nq)   CNBT

Quar Dec 31:	1999	1998
Net income..........	$1,302,000	$1,250,000
Shr earns (diluted):		
Net income	.27	.25
Year:		
Net income..........	4,956,000	4,485,000
Shr earns (basic):		
Net income	1.01	.89
Shr earns (diluted):		
Net income	1.00	.88

Catalina Marketing (N)   POS

Quar Dec 31:	1999	1998
Revenues..............	$97,790,000	$67,604,000
Net income..........	16,560,000	12,015,000
Avg dil shr	19,230,000	18,891,000
Shr earns (basic):		
Net income	.90	.65
Shr earns (diluted):		
Net income	.86	.64
9 months:		

Exploration Co. (Sc)   TXCO

Quar Nov 30:	1999	1998
Revenues..............	$2,994,942	$1,230,974
Net income..........	943,026	71,670
Avg dil shr	15,938,516	15,613,516
Shr earns (diluted):		
Net income	.06	.01

Fannie Mae (N)   FNM

Quar Dec 31:	1999	1998
Income $1,038,400,000		$899,300,000
aExtrd chg............	...	a(10,800,000)
Net income.......... 1,038,400,000		888,500,000
Avg dil shr 1,026,700,000		1,033,700,000
Shr earns (basic):		
Income............	1.00	.86
Net income	1.00	.85
Shr earns (diluted):		
Income............	.99	.85
Net income	.99	.84
Year:		
Income 3,921,100,000		3,444,400,000
aExtrd chg............	(9,200,000)	(26,300,000)
Net income.......... 3,911,900,000		3,418,100,000
Avg dil shr 1,030,700,000		1,037,400,000
Shr earns (basic):		
Income............	3.75	3.28
Net income	3.75	3.26
Shr earns (diluted):		
Income............	3.73	3.26
Net income	3.72	3.23
a-From early extinguishment of debt.		

First Bancorp-P.R. (N)   FBP

Quar Dec 31:	1999	1998
Net income..........	$16,332,000	$13,686,000
Shr earns (basic):		
Net income	.52	.46
Shr earns (diluted):		
Net income	.51	.46
Year:		
Net income..........	62,075,000	51,812,000
Shr earns (basic):		
Net income	2.00	1.75
Shr earns (diluted):		
Net income	1.98	1.74

EXHIBIT 17 Digest of Earnings Report (continued)

Loews Cineplex (N)   LCP

Quar Nov 30:	1999	1998
Revenues..............	$209,250,000	$211,414,000
aNet income.........	(23,838,000)	(12,106,000)
Avg dil shr	58,622,646	58,622,646
Shr earns (diluted):		
Net income......	(.41)	(.21)
9 months:		
Revenues..............	714,326,000	626,687,000
aNet income........	(29,854,000)	(4,575,000)
Avg dil shr	58,622,646	44,238,506
Shr earns (diluted):		
Net income......	(.51)	(.10)

a-Includes charges from the sale of assets of $2,411,000 in the quarter and $7,124,000 in the nine months of 1999 compared with $3,567,000 and $4,569,000, respectively, in 1998.

Marshall & Isley (N)   MI

Quar Dec 31:	1999	1998
Net income...........	$90,600,000	$83,470,000
Shr earns (diluted):		
Net income......	.81	.72
Year:		
Net income...........	354,500,000	a301,323,000
Shr earns (diluted):		
Net income......	3.14	2.61

a-Includes net nonrecurring charges of $16,268,000.

McCormick & Co. (N)   MKC

Quar Nov 30:	1999	1998
Sales....................	$620,435,000	$585,698,000
aNet income........	53,979,000	50,078,000
Avg dil shr	71,350,000	73,242,000
Shr earns (basic):		
Net income......	.76	.69
Shr earns (diluted):		
Net income......	.76	.68
Year:		
Sales....................	2,006,917,000	1,881,146,000
aNet income........	103,306,000	103,828,000
Avg dil shr	71,999,000	73,886,000
Shr earns (basic):		
Net income......	1.45	1.42
Shr earns (diluted):		

PNC Bank Corp. (N)   PNC

Quar Dec 31:	1999	1998
Net income.........	$304,000,000	$285,000,000
Avg dil shr	296,300,000	304,700,000
Shr earns (basic):		
Net income......	1.02	.93
Shr earns (diluted):		
Net income......	1.01	.92
Year:		
Net income.........	1,264,000,000	1,115,000,000
Avg dil shr	300,000,000	305,100,000
Shr earns (basic):		
Net income......	4.19	3.64
Shr earns (diluted):		
Net income......	4.15	3.60

Pacific Aero & El (Nq)   PCTH

Quar Nov 30:	1999	1998
Sales.....................	$29,000,000	$30,477,000
Net income...........	(2,014,000)	a(2,575,000)
Avg dil shr	19,992,000	16,731,000
Shr earns (diluted):		
Net income......	(.10)	(.15)
6 months:		
Sales.....................	57,551,000	49,655,000
Net income...........	(3,520,000)	a(6,986,000)
Avg dil shr	19,547,000	16,073,000
Shr earns (diluted):		
Net income......	(.18)	(.43)

a-Includes net nonrecurring charges of $1,600,000 in the quarter and $6,000,000 in the six months.

Precision Castpart (N)   PCP

13 wk Dec 26:	1999	1998
Sales.....................	$404,700,000	$361,200,000
Net income...........	a12,700,000	25,700,000
Shr earns (diluted):		
Net income......	.52	1.05
39 weeks:		
Sales....................	1,121,600,000	1,094,600,000
Net income...........	a58,300,000	75,400,000
Shr earns (basic):		
Net income......	2.38	3.10
Shr earns (diluted):		
Net income......	2.37	3.08

a-Includes nonrecurring charges of $11,000,000.

If companies possess a complex capital structure, a dual presentation of EPS is required. Accountants refer to these EPS figures as "basic earnings per share" and "diluted earnings per share." Where large amounts of convertible securities are present, the assumption of full dilution can significantly reduce EPS.

Conclusion. Investors must be careful not to rely too heavily on EPS as reported in the financial press. Details in the income statements, such as trends in gross margin, may be more important than EPS. In addition, EPS may reveal little about the financial condition and cash flows of the firm. This information is generally presented in the annual and quarterly reports that a corporation issues. However, EPS can often be a valuable guide to evaluating a single firm's comparative performance over time. Because EPS is affected by the choices of accounting methods, and one firm's choices may be quite different from those of another firm, comparisons of EPS between firms should be made with caution.

45

BALANCE SHEET

The balance sheet is a document that discloses the financial condition of a company at a particular point in time. This statement summarizes what a firm owns (assets), what a firm owes to outsiders (liabilities), and the interests of the owners of the enterprise (owners' equity or stockholders' equity). In equation form, the balance sheet can be represented as follows:

$$Assets \ = \ Liabilities \ + \ stockholders' \ equity$$

By definition, the balance sheet must always balance, meaning the total balance for assets must always equal the total balance of the sum of liabilities and stockholders' equity. Thus, when a corporation increases its assets or decreases its liabilities, stockholders' equity grows.

Assets can be divided into three major categories:

1. *Current assets:* Cash plus other assets generally expected to be converted into cash within one year, e.g., inventories and receivables
2. *Property, plant, and equipment:* Assets with relatively long lives
3. *Intangible assets:* Valuable rights that have no physical substance, such as patents and copyrights

Balanced against assets are liabilities, which are economic obligations of two types: current (generally payable within one year) and long-term.

Financial Ratios. Many financial ratios that are widely reported in the financial press are computed based upon the values on the balance sheet.

- *Book value per share:* Book value is defined as a company's total assets less its total liabilities. Many investors look for undervalued companies and possible takeover candidates by buying stocks that are selling at a low price relative to book value. They typically focus upon "tangible" book value, excluding such intangibles as patents and goodwill. This value becomes less relevant if the valuations on the balance sheet do not approximate the current market value of the assets.
- *Debt ratio:* This value is computed by dividing total liabilities by total assets. This ratio indicates the extent of the firm's financing with debt. The use of debt involves risk because it requires fixed interest payments and eventual repayment of principal. Particular attention should be paid to the debt ratio when considering troubled companies. Debt is a primary determinant of which companies will survive and which will go bankrupt in a crisis.
- *Current ratio:* This ratio is the most commonly used measure of short-run liquidity, calculated by dividing current assets by current liabilities. This ratio gives an indication of the company's ability over the next 12 months to meet its obligations and still have sufficient resources to run its business effectively. There is no single "correct" current ratio; the figure varies from industry to industry.

46

MERGERS AND ACQUISITIONS

A merger occurs when one firm absorbs another firm and the latter loses its corporate identity. The terms *mergers* and *acquisitions* are now used interchangeably on Wall Street. There are many different ways to effect business combinations. Deals may involve stock acquisition, asset acquisition, or a combination of the two. In a stock acquisition, the acquiring firm (or individual) obtains controlling interest in the voting stock of the acquired firm and absorbs that firm. In an asset acquisition, the acquiring firm directly purchases the assets of the acquired firm. "Merger" is often combined with "acquisitions" and abbreviated as M&As. When "takeover" is used in the context of M&As, it implies that the acquired firm's management opposed the acquisition.

Current Merger and Acquisition Activity. The total value of acquisitions increased from a paltry $58 billion in 1992 to $3.4 trillion worldwide in 1999, with no letup in sight. Deals of unprecedented size and involving companies of global scope were announced almost weekly. For example, in October 1999, Sprint announced that it was acquiring MCI WorldCom in a deal worth $115 billion. No doubt the heady heights of stock prices have something to do with this activity. In the mid-1990s, the average price-earnings ratio in the United States stood at about 18, based upon earnings for the previous four quarters. By 1999, that ratio had increased to over 30. Higher stock prices enabled companies to pay more for acquisitions.

The telecommunications sector was a fertile area for mergers—particularly megamergers. The Sprint combination with MCI WorldCom was the first to crack the $100 billion barrier. Telecom mergers accounted for 16% of all mergers and acquisitions in 1999.

Look for the trend in megamergers to continue in the next decade. The Internet is revolutionizing the way business is being conducted. E-commerce among businesses is expected to catapult from $114 billion in 1999 to $1.5 trillion by 2004. Many traditional companies will have to remake themselves to meet new consumer demands. The push to increase efficiency will continue to drive mergers and acquisitions in the future.

The announcement in January 2000 that America Online (AOL), the world's biggest online company, agreed to buy Time Warner, the world's biggest media company, for about $160 billion confirms the triumph of the Internet as an irresistible force in business. The possibilities for combinations are limitless—and it's not just Internet and media companies. We will see many more mergers of Internet firms with traditional brick-and-mortar companies.

In order to gain control of a company, a buyout specialist will generally make a tender offer to all the stockholders of a company to purchase a specified number of shares at a specified price within a specified time frame. The offer may come from the company itself or from another company or investor group. Tender offers are often part of hostile takeovers. The tender offer price is generally substantially above the current price to encourage shareholders to tender their shares. The stock price will spurt in response to the tender offer, but will settle at a level slightly below the tender offer price. This gap arises because of the possibility that the takeover may fail.

Arbitrageurs often dominate the trading in a stock for which a tender offer has been made. These speculators try to buy a stock for less than they will ultimately be paid by the acquirer. This type of activity is typically conducted by market professionals and not individual investors.

Takeover Terminology. Takeover mania in the 1980s has spawned a colorful vocabulary, mostly reflecting the efforts of companies to fend off corporate raiders. Some terms that have become commonly used in the financial press are *poison pill*, a tactic designed to make a hostile takeover more expensive; *white knight*, a person or corporation who saves a corporation from a hostile takeover by taking the company over on friendlier terms; *golden parachute*, lucrative severance pay or stock allowances for top executives concerned about their positions; *greenmail*, a concept similar to blackmail that refers to a corporation's buying back stock from a potential acquirer at a price that substantially exceeds the going market price; and *shark repellent*, wherein a potential takeover target enhances its defenses by the inclusion of corporate bylaws designed to put obstacles in the path of a takeover.

Leveraged Buyouts. A leveraged buyout (LBO) is a type of acquisition undertaken by a firm's managers with financing from a bank or investment group. Essentially, management buys the company's shares with borrowed money. Debts are paid from the company's cash flow. In addition, parts of the acquired company may be sold off to reduce debt. The term *leveraged* is appropriate because the majority of the new company's capitalization is debt. Later, the firm's stock may be sold to the public again or to another investment group, often producing tremendous profits for the managers and their bankers. If successful, the financial rewards can be awesome. The investors who put $80 million into Dr Pepper in 1986 received more than $600 million in cash in 1988.

47

INVESTMENT SCAMS

Every year the financial media report on an investment scam that has duped unwary investors. Investors continue to put their money in scams that clearly ought to arouse suspicion. In 2000, affinity groups fraud is a serious concern. This type of fraud is perpetrated on religious, ethnic, and professional groups by members of these groups or persons enjoying the trust of these groups.

Ponzi Schemes. A 30-year-old immigrant, Charles Ponzi, etched his name in the annals of history in 1920 when he made an offer thousands of investors could not refuse: a 50% return in just six weeks. By the time the scheme began to unravel six months later, Ponzi had pocketed $10 million. His name has become synonymous with confidence games in which some early investors earn excellent returns, paid off with funds obtained from later participants in a scheme, who lose everything. Variations on the Ponzi scheme have duped investors over and over again. When the demand for new participants exhausts the supply, the Ponzi pyramid collapses, crushing the hopes of its "investors." The lesson here is to be skeptical about a guarantee of far higher interest rates or returns than that prevailing in the marketplace.

Stock Scams. Any investment that guarantees an unusually high rate of return should be regarded as suspect. The penny stock market, which consists of stocks selling for less than $1 per share, has been a continuing source of headaches to securities regulators. Investors are bilked by swindlers who prey on those who substitute greed for sound judgment. The emergence of computerized dialing and cheap long-distance phone rates has allowed smooth-talking brokers working out of "boiler rooms" to contact millions of people. They offer stock in small companies for a few cents per share, promising huge profits in a short time. Investors should be wary of the penny stock market.

Internet Fraud. Both the SEC and North American Securities Administrators Association (NASAA) have identified Internet fraud as a major area of concern. The SEC now gets as many as 300 e-mails per day from investors reporting potential Internet frauds, up from just a dozen three years ago. The NASAA has uncovered a wide variety of scams using the Internet, including stock price manipulation, illegal pyramid schemes, insider trading, and acting as a broker or investment adviser without proper licensure.

Phony Financial Planners. A growing number of crooks are exploiting individuals concerned about their financial well-being by selling them bogus investments and worthless counseling. Most of this fraud is not perpetrated by financial planners, but by individuals posing as financial planners. Investors can reduce their chances of falling prey to a charlatan by checking the backgrounds of financial planners and other professionals with the National Association of Securities Dealers' Public Disclosure web site (*www.nasdr.com/2000.htm*). Requests for information generally can be processed in five to ten days. The cost for businesses is $30; the service is free to individuals.

Several web sites are available to assist investors in avoiding scams and dubious investments. *StockDetective.com* alerts users to Wall Street "No Gooders" who are targets of SEC actions. This site also presents "Stinky Stocks," targeting companies with stocks of questionable value. Another useful site is *www.nasdr.com*, which contains disclosure information on licensed brokers and member firms, including records of disciplinary and enforcement actions. Finally, the NASAA operates a web site, *www.nasaa.org*, that provides educational investor protection material along with links to various regulatory agencies, as well as investor protection groups.

48

ASSET ALLOCATION

Most investors believe that the most important investing decision they make is the selection of individual stocks, bonds, mutual funds, and so forth. However, these decisions are not nearly as important as generally assumed. The asset allocation decision—how you split your dollars among stocks, bonds, and cash (including money market funds and short-term CDs)—is by far the most important determinant of investment performance. The portion of your total assets invested in stocks is generally far more important than the individual stocks you select.

Although the importance of asset allocation over individual security selection may surprise you, this concept is not news to the academics who researched this issue. One study, by Brinson, Singer, and Beebower (published in the May–June 1991 issue of *Financial Analysts Journal*), assessed the performance of 82 large pension funds over a ten-year period. Their research shows that asset allocation determines more than 90% of the variation in total return. The individual stocks and the other assets that the pension funds picked did little on average to improve performance over the ten-year period.

Many investment advisers in recent years have increasingly emphasized asset allocation as an approach to investment. Although this approach might be perceived as a gimmick to sell financial products, investors can ignore allocation only at their own peril.

Most investors tend to pay little or no attention to how they allocate their assets. All too often, they own a hodge-podge of mutual funds or common stock bought at various times without consideration of how they complement each other. This approach is a big mistake.

Proper attention to asset allocation can enable you to substantially enhance your return with little or no increase in risk.

The 30-year compound annual total return (1970–1999), including price changes and reinvested dividends, for common stock (as measured by the Standard & Poor's 500 Index) is 12.5%. But the average return masks some years of glittering returns and other years that were real downers. Total returns soared more than 30% in seven of the years, but stocks were losing investments in six other years, including the 26.47% plunge in 1974. Some investors may not be comfortable with the level of volatility or risk. Those investors who plan to cash in their stocks to finance the college education of their children or for their retirement in a few years may find the possibility of a 26.47% plunge unacceptable.

That's where asset allocation helps. Consider what would have happened if an investor had put one third of his or her money in stocks, one third in Treasury bonds, and one third in a cash equivalent such as Treasury bills. In the 30-year period, that investor would have lost money only four times, and the largest loss would have been less than 5%. Meanwhile, the compound annual return over the 30 years would have been 10%, compared with 12.5% for an all-stock portfolio. Thus, historically, sacrificing a 2.5% total return has been accompanied by dramatically reduced risk.

If you are interested in making the most money possible, and your time horizon is 30 to 40 years, then investing entirely in stocks makes sense. Although you have a 30% chance of loss in any 1-year period (based on results over the last 60 years), your risk drops to 7% over any 5-year period and only 3% in any 10-year period. In other words, extending the amount of time invested in the stock market greatly reduces risk.

But most investors have shorter time horizons, and investing totally in stocks is too risky. For them, investing in several classes of assets such as stocks, bonds, real estate (at least your own home), and cash equivalents is a better approach.

Because asset mix is so important, some mutual fund companies now offer free services to help investors design their portfolios. These companies include Fidelity (*www.fidelity.com*), Vanguard (*www.vanguard.com*), Strong (*www.strong.funds.com*), and Berger (*www.bergerfunds.com*). They either suggest an allocation upon completion of a questionnaire or provide a worksheet that assists in figuring out the appropriate mix.

For an excellent discussion of asset allocation, as well as investing in general, consider *SmartMoney*'s web site at *www.smartmoney.com*. This site also provides a worksheet, which helps tailor an asset mix to the investor's particular needs.

The best combinations of investments vary depending upon age, income, health, employment stability, family size, and tolerance of risk. Each investor has to structure a strategy that fits his or her own personal circumstances, and this strategy will change as you get older and your financial position changes.

The evidence is convincing that stocks should constitute a substantial proportion of all long-term *financial portfolios*. What percentage should stocks be of a financial portfolio? There is an old rule of thumb that stocks, as a percentage of a portfolio, should equal 100 minus the investor's age. That standard is okay, but a portfolio allocation should be based upon risk tolerance and time horizon, and not only on age. Even 65-year-olds need to plan for inflation 15 to 20 years into their future.

A better rule would be to divide goals into short-term (less than three years), intermediate (three to ten years), and long-term (more than ten years). Money needed in three years can be put in money market funds or certificates of deposit (CDs). For intermediate goals, 60% stocks and 40% income investments would be a good mix. If planning beyond ten years, a diversified portfolio of common stocks makes sense. Those investors not comfortable doing their own stock picking should buy highly diversified mutual funds with low expense ratios. Index funds, in particular, have these characteristics.

When looking at how assets are allocated, all investments should be considered, including real estate, brokerage accounts, 401(k) money, individual retirement accounts, and certificates of deposit. After an investor has settled upon the mix of investments desired, maintenance of the desired percentage for the mix is all that is needed. To accomplish this goal, the allocation should be computed at least once a year. Downturns in the stock market can cause stocks to become a smaller percentage of the financial portfolio than desired. In that case, more cash should be put into stocks.

49

SOURCES OF INFORMATION

The purpose of this Key is to describe the primary sources of information available to assist investors in making investment decisions. An investor does not need to read all the sources to make an informed choice. However, one should be aware of trends in the economy and business activity. Most successful investors have a broad knowledge of the business and investment environment, so that they are capable of making judgments independent of the so-called experts. Such knowledge is important because the opinions of experts are frequently contradictory.

The most accessible source of information for nearly all investors is the financial section of a newspaper. Newspapers vary from excellent to poor in their coverage of financial developments. The *New York Times* has an excellent financial section and is widely available. Many investors also choose to supplement their local newspapers with a specialized financial newspaper such as the *Wall Street Journal*, by far the most widely read daily of its type. *Investor's Business Daily* is also useful, particularly to those investors who use technical analysis.

There also are many general business periodicals and financial magazines available. *Business Week*, *Fortune*, and *Forbes* are three major business magazines. *Business Week* is more oriented toward news reporting. In contrast, *Forbes* and *Fortune* (both published biweekly) focus on specific companies and business personalities. Investors should examine these periodicals and subscribe to at least one that appears most useful in enhancing their understanding of the stock market. *Barron's*, the weekly sister publication of the *Wall Street Journal*, provides a wealth of useful financial data as well as columns and features on events significant to investors. *Money* carries many articles on investments and is a useful source of information on all aspects of financial planning. Incidentally, all of these publications have excellent web sites.

Statistical Services. Standard & Poor's (S&P) provides a broad array of products covering the entire investment arena. With respect to stocks, S&P publishes a monthly *Stock Guide*, the weekly *Outlook*, and a series of individual stock reports available at brokerage firms. These one-page reports provide a useful summary and description of a company's operations and financial history.

S&P has an excellent personal investment web site at *www.personalwealth.com*. The monthly subscription of $9.95 includes 20 *Enhanced Analytics* per month, or they may be purchased for $1 each.

Another excellent advisory service is the *Value Line Investment Survey*, a publication providing a one-page summary of useful financial data on individual companies. This publication also provides separate rankings on a 1 to 5 scale of timeliness and safety. *Timeliness* is the probable price performance relative to the market over the upcoming 12 months. *Safety* is the stock's future price stability and the company's current financial strength, where a rank of 1 is the highest. This systematized approach tells the investor exactly how *Value Line* regards the prospects of each company. (Descriptions of other advisory services are discussed in Key 35.)

Direct from the Company. Before buying stock in a company, an investor should gather all the information he or she can from the company itself. The phone number can be found by checking the company's web site or a web site like Yahoo!Finance (*www.quote.yahoo.com*); click the "profile" button for a telephone number. In response to phone queries, shareholder relations will send an annual report, Form 10-Q, and a proxy statement upon request. The contact person typically will direct the caller to the company's web site as well.

The *annual report* is the formal report issued yearly by a corporation to its stockholders. The report includes the president's letter, management's discussion and analysis of operations, balance sheet, income statement, statement of cash flows, note disclosures, and the report of the independent auditors.

Form 10-Q is a quarterly update to the annual report, containing condensed financial information that updates the company's financial position and results of operations for the quarter.

The *proxy statement* provides information about items to be voted on at the annual meeting. In addition, it provides information about management and directors not available in other reports to stockholders. Of particular interest is the number of shares owned by officers and directors. These data are important because, in general, the greater their ownership of common stock, the more likely their interests are aligned with those of the stockholders.

Companies must transmit a Form 10-K (similar to the annual report), Form 10-Q, and proxy statements to the SEC. The SEC makes those forms available on its web site (*www.sec.gov/edgarhp.htm*), which unfortunately is not very user-friendly. A better way to tap into this information is to use the web site called FreeEdgar (*www.freeedgar.com*).

Books. One of the best books ever written on investing in common stocks is Jeremy Siegel's *Stocks for the Long Run* (McGraw-Hill, 1998). John Bogle's *Common Sense on Mutual Funds* (John Wiley & Sons, 1999) is the most insightful book on investing in mutual funds. *Trading the Fundamentals* by Niemira and Zukowski (McGraw-Hill, 1998) is an excellent guide to understanding economic indicators and their effect on the financial markets.

50

FINANCIAL WEB SITES

The biggest difference between this edition of the book and the previous edition written five years ago is the stunning amount of information available to the individual investor. The Internet offers the individual investor an immense amount of data that were available only to professionals just a few years ago. With more than 10,000 web sites devoted to the topics of investing, the sheer volume of information can be intimidating, and much of it has little value. However, there are numerous web sites that can help investors make decisions. The selections we have chosen are ones that we have found to be particularly useful.

Home Base. Many web sites are trying to be the first stop for stock research. However, a quick check of these financial "portals" discloses that much of the data originates from the same set of providers, such as Zack's and First Call for earnings estimates and Reuters for news. Because of the redundancy, choosing where to begin is a matter of personal preference.

Yahoo!Finance (www.quote.yahoo.com). Our current favorite starting point is Yahoo!Finance. With a clear, well-designed layout, Yahoo!Finance provides a wealth of answers obtainable with a single click. Along with delayed stock quotes (15 minutes for Nasdaq stocks, 20 minutes otherwise), Yahoo!Finance is a comprehensive news source that includes the following feeds: Reuters Financial News, PR Newswire, Standard & Poor's Business Wire, Zack's, company profiles, and mutual fund profiles. New feeds and services are being added regularly.

Microsoft Investor (www.investor.com). This site,

which used to cost $9.95 a month, is now available without charge. For those interested in news, this site includes items from MSNBC and Reuters as well as Investor staff reports, which are updated three times daily. The "Insight" section has regular columnists who provide some of the best investment commentary on the Web. Want to buy a stock or fund? The investor can screen 16,000 stocks and funds in over 500 criteria to find just the right ones. They have also created 20 preset stock and fund screens to make getting started easy.

The Wall Street Journal Interactive Edition (www.wsj.com). Here is the way to have the leading business newspaper, the *Wall Street Journal*, continuously updated. The quality of the information accessible is what makes this web site a standout. Subscribers are provided continuous news coverage, searchable archives, and access to detailed company data. Breaking news on topics and investments of the subscriber's choice are available.

CBS Market Watch (cbs.marketwatch.com). *CBS Market Watch*, a joint venture between CBS and market information provider DBC, has a large staff providing original market news and commentary throughout the day. The web site includes quotes, mutual fund data, charting, and portfolio tracking—at absolutely no cost.

FreeEDGAR (www.freeedgar.com). All publicly traded companies have to submit a Form 10-K (annual report) and a Form 10-Q (quarterly report) to the SEC. This information is easier to access by using FreeEdgar rather than the SEC's web site (*www.sec.gov*). Also, users can register to have e-mail alerts when their own companies file with the SEC.

Quicken.com (www.quicken.com). This great, all-purpose web site includes stock market commentary, simple and useful search tools for stocks and funds, earnings estimates, and insider trading information. As the maker of the world's most popular investment software, Quicken has made this web site user-friendly. The investment section includes not only stock and fund data, but also information on insurance, taxes, and retirement planning. Best of all, it's *free*.

The Motley Fool (www.fool.com). This web site, created by the Gardner brothers, is dedicated to making investing easier. The Fool offers a 13-step program to educate beginning investors. Graduates are taught more sophisticated techniques, such as using screens to find fast-growing companies and tracking the latest favorites of the momentum followers. This free web site also offers excellent summaries of the quarterly conference calls that major companies conduct with Wall Street analysts.

Federal Reserve Bank of Chicago (www.frbchi.org). The Chicago Branch of the Federal Reserve is an excellent site for those interested in following the Federal Reserve in particular and the economy in general. This site contains a wealth of economic and financial data, including some informative tutorials on basic economic terms.

The Dismal Scientist (www.dismal.com). A really nifty, user-friendly site we highly recommend is the Dismal Scientist. A calendar lists the economic releases with a discussion of each indicator and disclosure of the forecasted numbers. Included are illuminating articles on current economic issues, as well as longer-term analyses of economic trends. The site even includes a calculator to find out if the stock market is fairly valued.

QUESTIONS AND ANSWERS

What do the terms EPS and P/E mean?

EPS, *earnings per share*, is calculated by subtracting preferred stock dividends from net income and dividing the remainder by the average number of common shares outstanding for the year. Annual EPS is often considered a summary indicator because it presents substantial information on the firm's performance in a single item.

If there are any extraordinary gains or losses in the year, that portion of EPS is calculated separately to eliminate the distortion they may lend to the annual earnings. If a firm has issued convertible securities or other financial instruments that can be exchanged for or converted into common shares, EPS must be computed to show the possible dilution of EPS by such conversions.

Investors must be careful not to rely too heavily on EPS because details such as gross margin on sales, working capital ratios, and cash flows are not reflected in EPS. Therefore, EPS is more valuable as a guide to evaluating a firm's performance over time than as a basis for comparison among different firms.

P/E is price-earnings ratio, which is the market price of a stock divided by its annual EPS. Thus, P/E is a good indicator of how investors regard a company's (or the overall market's) prospects. Growth stocks generally have higher P/Es than the shares of public utilities, for example, and P/Es in general are higher in bull markets than in bear markets

What advantages do dividend reinvestment plans have for investors?

Those investors who wish to buy shares of common stock as cheaply as possible have an alternative: dividend reinvestment plans (DRIPs). More than 1,100 companies offer DRIPs, and the number continues to increase every year. DRIPs are tailor-made for long-term buy-and-hold investors.

What do the primary stock market averages and indexes measure?

The Dow Jones Industrial Average is the average most widely followed by individual investors. The 30 corporations measured by DJIA are large "blue-chip" companies. The stock averages are price-weighted, meaning that the component stock prices are added together and divided by a particular divisor.

The Standard & Poor's 500 Index (also called the Composite Index) is the index most widely followed by market professionals. On a daily basis, it is more representative of the movement of the stock market as a whole because it uses a larger sample of 500 stocks. It is a market-weighted index, which means a stock's price change is proportional to the issue's overall market value (share price times the number of shares outstanding).

The Nasdaq Composite Index is a market-weighted index composed of all domestic and foreign stocks on the Nasdaq. High-technology stocks now comprise more than 70% of the market value of the Nasdaq.

The Russell 2000 Index is a market-weighted index that tracks the 2,000 smallest companies in the Russell universe of 3,000 companies. This index is widely considered the benchmark for small-company stocks.

What is a 401(k) plan?

A 401(k) plan is a retirement plan that permits employees to defer paying taxes on a part of their salary. This contribution is deducted from your salary and is not counted as part of earnings for current income tax purposes. The plan provides employees with an automatic way to save for retirement, while reducing and deferring taxes.

How does financial leverage benefit a company?

Financial leverage is the use of debt to magnify returns. Speculators attempt to magnify returns by supplementing their own funds with borrowed funds. Companies also use leverage to increase income. Like individuals, they use debt to increase the resources available to generate future profits. Leveraging is successful as long as the money borrowed produces returns greater than the interest charges on the additional debt incurred. However, debt increases risk because a company commits itself to making fixed-interest payments. A company that does not meet its interest payments generally becomes insolvent.

What is the difference between a bull market and a bear market? What are the implications of each to an investor?

A bull market is a prolonged rise in the price of stocks; a bear market is a prolonged decline in the price of stocks. Historical studies indicate that 60% of stock price movements are directly related to movements in the overall market; 30% to 35% are related to sector or group movements; and only about 5% are related to individual stock movements.

What does diversification mean? What is the simplest way to diversify?

Diversification can substantially reduce investment risk. Diversification can be thought of as "not putting all your eggs into one basket." An effectively diversified portfolio reduces risk without cutting long-run average return.

In selecting stocks, investors should be careful to select stocks that do not follow the same pattern in response to changes in economic variables.

What does the Index of Leading Economic Indicators tell me?

The index can provide valuable information about the future path of the economy. It generally grows at a rate of 3% per year, about the same rate as the economy. If the index declines for several consecutive months, it is an indicator that a recession may be forthcoming. Conversely, if the index grows faster than 3%, rapid growth in the future may be expected. There are short-comings in the index, and many argue that a broader index should be constructed. Most importantly, it should be noted that long-term trends in the index are far more indicative of movement in the economy than are any month-to-month fluctuations.

When are stocks assets on the balance sheet and when are they stockholders' equity?

When a corporation holds shares of another company's stock as an investment, the holding is classified as an asset. Whether it is classified as a current asset or a long-term investment depends upon the intent of management. For it to be a current asset, the intent must be to sell it within the next year.

GLOSSARY

Acquisition   combination of firms in which the acquiring firm obtains controlling interest in the voting stock of the acquired firm.

Assets   economic resources expected to provide future benefits to a firm.

Balance sheet   provides information about the assets, liabilities, and owners' equity of a company as of a particular date.

Bear market   prolonged decrease in the prices of common stocks.

Bond ratings   system of evaluating the credit quality of bonds by assigning the bonds to different risk classifications.

Bull market   prolonged increase in the prices of common stocks.

Call option   right of a buyer to purchase a specified quantity of a security interest at a fixed price at any time during the life of the option.

Closed-end fund   a fund that offers a fixed number of shares that are traded on exchanges like stocks and bonds.

Commodity futures   agreement to purchase or sell a specific amount of a commodity at a particular price on a stipulated future date.

Common stock   fractional shares of ownership interest in a corporation.

Consumer Price Index   a measure of prices at the consumer level for a fixed basket of goods and services.

Convertible security   a bond or share of preferred stock that can be exchanged into a specified amount of common stock at a specified price.

Corporate bond   long-term IOU of a corporation, secured by specific assets or a promise to pay; generally issued in units of $1,000.

Coupon rate (stated rate)   specified rate of interest that a corporation will pay its bondholders, expressed as an annual percentage of face value.

Deficit   the amount by which outlays and expenditures exceed receipts and revenues.

Diamonds   index products that trade on the AMEX and track the Dow Jones Industrial Average.

Discount rate   rate of interest charged by the Federal Reserve to member banks.

Dividend   payment to stockholders distributed from a corporation's earnings.

Earnings per share   amount of net income attributable to each share of common stock.

Face value (par value, maturity value)   amount the corporation must repay on the maturity due.

Federal funds rate   interest rate paid by banks when borrowing from other banks' reserves.

Federal Reserve System   central bank of the United States, which formulates monetary policy and controls the money supply.

Financial ratios   indicators of a company's financial performance and position.

Foreign exchange rate   price at which one currency can be traded for another.

Fundamental analysis   process of estimating a security's value by analyzing the basic financial and economic facts about the company.

Golden parachute   lucrative compensation guaranteed top executives in the event of a takeover.

Greenmail   purchase by a corporation of its own stock from a potential acquirer at a price substantially greater than the market price. In exchange, the acquirer agrees to drop the takeover bid.

Gross domestic product   measurement of economic activity by computing the total market value of all goods and services produced in a given period.

Holding company   investment company that owns a substantial ownership interest in other companies.

Income statement   financial statement that shows a firm's revenues and expenses over a period of time.

Initial public offering (IPO)   corporation's first offering of its own stock to the public.

Investment banking   the industry that specializes in assisting business firms and governments in marketing new security issues.

iShares   *see* WEBS.

Junk bond   a high-risk, high-yield bond (less than BBB rating).

Leverage   accelerative effect of debt on financial returns.

Leveraged buyout (LBO)   process of buying a corporation's stock with borrowed money, then repaying the debt from the corporation's assets.

Liabilities   economic obligations of the firm to outsiders.

Liquidity   the ease with which an asset can be converted into cash, reflecting a firm's ability to meet its short-term obligations.

Load fund   type of mutual fund where the buyer must pay a sales fee, or commission, on top of the price.

Margin   in securities, the amount of cash down payment and money borrowed from a broker to purchase stocks; in futures, a deposit of money that can be used by the broker to cover losses that may occur in trading futures.

Maturity   date at which the principal amount of a bond is to be paid to the bondholder.

Merger   combination of two or more firms into one.

Monetarist   person who believes that the Federal Reserve's monetary policy, and not the government's fiscal policy, can control future levels of economic activity.

Monetary policy   actions by the Federal Reserve to control the money supply, bank lending, and interest rates.

Money market mutual funds   funds that invest in short-term debt instruments.

Money supply   sum total of money in an economy, including currency held by the public plus transaction accounts in depository institutions and travelers' checks.

Municipal bond   tax-exempt security issued by state and local governments and local government agencies and authorities.

Mutual funds   pool of commingled funds contributed by investors and managed by professional managers for a fee.

Nasdaq   National Association of Securities Dealers Automated Quotations; a computerized communications network that provides automated quotations (bid and ask prices) on stock.

Net asset value   calculated by dividing the total assets of a fund by the number of mutual shares outstanding.

No-load fund   type of mutual fund for which no fee is charged when it is initially issued.

Nominal interest rate   rate of interest expressed in current dollars (not deflated for price level changes).

Open-end mutual fund   fund that issues more shares as investors purchase more shares at a price equal to net asset value.

Over-the-counter market   trades securities through a centralized computer telephone network that links dealers across the United States.

Poison pill   tactic used by corporations to defend against unfriendly takeovers, generally by making a takeover more expensive.

Preferred stock   class of stock that has certain preferential rights over common stock.

Price-earnings ratio   ratio of a share's market price to a company's earnings per share.

Prime rate   interest rate charged by banks to their most creditworthy customers.

Productivity   measure of the efficiency in the use of economic resources.

Put option   right of buyer to sell a specified quantity of a security interest at a fixed price at any time during the life of the option.

Real interest rate   nominal rate of interest less the anticipated rate of inflation.

Secondary offering   any sale of additional common stock after the initial public offering.

Securities and Exchange Commission   U.S. government agency that administers the federal laws that protect the investor.

Spiders   index products that track Standard & Poor's 500 Stock Index and are traded on the AMEX.

Statement of cash flows   financial statement that shows a firm's cash receipts and payments over a period of time.

Stock dividend   pro rata distribution of additional shares of stock to stockholders.

Stock market average   index of the market prices of a specified number of stocks.

Stock table   summary of the trading activity of individual securities.

Strike price   exercise price, the price at which the stock or commodity underlying an option may be bought or sold.

Tender offer   offer by one firm to the stockholders of another firm to purchase a specified number of shares at a specified price within a specified time frame.

Trade deficit   amount by which the value of merchandise imports exceeds the value of exports.

Treasury securities   debt obligations issued by the U.S. government and backed by the full faith and credit of the government.

Warrant   option to buy a specified number of common shares at a predetermined price within a fixed time period.

WEBS   shares traded on the AMEX that efficiently track selected international equity markets. (Now called iShares.)

White knight   person or company that saves a corporation from a hostile takeover by taking it over on more favorable terms.

INDEX

171